STD

ACPL ITEM

DISCARDED

3 1833 00029 7433

Y0-AAW-455

Y 2

GOTTSCHALK, ALFRED

TO LEARN AND TO TEACH

DO NOT REMOVE
CARDS FROM POCKET

ALLEN COUNTY PUBLIC LIBRARY

FORT WAYNE, INDIANA 46802

You may return this book to any agency, branch,
or bookmobile of the Allen County Public Library.

TO LEARN AND
TO TEACH:
Your Life as a Rabbi

Rabbi Alfred Gottschalk, Ph.D.
S.T.D., D. Litt., D.Hu.L., L.L.D.,
D.Relig. Ed.

Revised by
Rabbi Gary P. Zola

THE ROSEN PUBLISHING GROUP, INC.
NEW YORK

Allen County Public Library
Ft. Wayne, Indiana

Published in 1988 by The Rosen Publishing Group, Inc.
29 East 21st Street, New York, NY 10010

Copyright 1988 by Rabbi Alfred Gottschalk

All rights reserved. No part of this book may be reproduced in any form without permission in writing from the publisher, except by a reviewer.
First Edition

Library of Congress Cataloging-in-Publication Data

Gottschalk, Alfred.
To learn and to teach.

Bibliography: p. 111
Includes index.
1. Rabbis – United States – Office. I. Title.
BM652.G62   1987   296.6′1   87–12904
ISBN 0–8239–0700–7

Manufactured in the United States of America

In Acknowledgment

This volume is published under the joint sponsorship of

The Scheuer Family Foundation
and the
Adolph Feibel Memorial Fund for Leadership Development

Appreciation

The author would like to express sincere appreciation to those whose generous assistance made the revision of this book so much easier: Rabbi Morris Allen, JTS; Rabbi Chaim Bronstein, RIETS; Richard Cohen, UAHC; Rabbi Barry H. Greene, Commission on Jewish Chaplaincy; Rabbi Jules Harlow, RA; Rabbi Richard Hirsch, RRC; Rabbi Abraham Isaac Ingber, Association of Hillel and Jewish Campus Professionals; Dr. Abraham Peck, American Jewish Archives; Ruth M. Perry, USA; Rabbi Herschel Schacter, RIETS; Dr. Jonathan D. Sarna, HUC-JIR; Dr. Ida Selavan, HUC-JIR; Helen Simon, Yeshiva University; Rabbi Donald M. Splansky, Temple Beth Am, Framingham, Massachusetts; Rabbi Elliot Stevens, CCAR; Rabbi Gordon Tucker, JTS.

A double portion of gratitude goes to a few special persons who committed themselves to this effort as if it were their very own: Lisa B. Frankel, Donna Swillinger, and Debra Poulter, who cheerfully typed and retyped the manuscript, and Student Rabbis Susan Miller and Kathy Schwartz, whose able research assistance made work on the Bibliographic Essay much less tedious.

Finally, my thanks go to Rabbi Gary Zola, my colleague and friend, who agreed to revise this book out of his perceived need as National Director of Admissions and Student Affairs at HUC-JIR that such a book should be current and on the shelves of libraries and rabbis' studies to encourage the Jewish idealist to consider the rabbinate as a life's calling. He has fulfilled his task with care and devotion.

About the Author

Rabbi Alfred Gottschalk, President of Hebrew Union College-Jewish Institute of Religion, is one of the current generation of college and university presidents who are reshaping higher education in the United States.

The College-Institute, the oldest institution of Jewish higher education in America, has campuses in Cincinnati, New York, Los Angeles, and Jerusalem. It is primarily a graduate institution training Reform rabbis, cantors, educators, and communal workers and preparing advanced students—Christian as well as Jewish—for academic careers.

Before assuming the presidency of the College-Institute in 1971, Dr. Gottschalk was dean of its California school, which he built from very modest beginnings into an impressive academic and educational center.

Under his leadership the first woman rabbi was ordained and the number of women admitted to the professional and academic programs of the HUC-JIR increased dramatically. Traditionally, women were barred from the rabbinate. Today, most of the 115 women ordained by him are serving in rabbinic capacities or in related fields. Dr. Gottschalk also pioneered the School of Jewish Communal Service in Los Angeles and developed a program for the training of Progressive Rabbis at the College's Jerusalem School.

Born in Oberwesel, Germany, on March 7, 1930, Rabbi Gottschalk came to America as a youngster with his parents fleeing from Nazi Germany. He received an A.B. degree from Brooklyn College and continued his studies at the New York and Cincinnati schools of the College-Institute, where in 1957 he was ordained Rabbi. He received a Ph.D. at the University of Southern California in 1965.

Dr. Gottschalk is active in many religious, cultural, and

secular organizations. He serves on the executive committees of the Central Conference of American Rabbis, the National Association of Temple Educators, and the Board of Trustees of the Union of American Hebrew Congregations. He is a Vice President of the World Union for Progressive Judaism and Chairman of the International Center for the Study of Jewish Civilization. Among his academic affiliations are membership in the American Association of Presidents of Independent Colleges and Universities, the American Philosophical Society, the Israel Exploration Society, the Society of Biblical Literature, the Board of Trustees of the Albright Institute of Archaeological Research, the Board of Trustees of the American Schools of Oriental Research, and many others.

Rabbi Gottschalk has received honorary degrees from the University of Southern California, The Jewish Theological Seminary, Dropsie University, The University of Judaism, the University of Cincinnati, Loyola Marymount University, Xavier University, St. Thomas Institute, and New York University. He is also an honorary Fellow of the Hebrew University. He is currently a member of the United States Holocaust Memorial Council.

Dr. Gottschalk is a leading researcher on the life and thoughts of Ahad Ha-Am, the founder of spiritual Zionism. He has published extensive works on Jewish thought and the status of contemporary Jewish life. Dr. Gottschalk is listed in *Who's Who in the World* and in *American Jewish Biographies*. He has served on the Editorial Advisory Board of *American Jewish Biographies* and on the Editorial Board of the *Hebrew Union College Annual*.

Contents

Introduction to the Revised Edition

Browsing in the reference section of my high school's library one day some years ago, I noticed a colorfully bounded, newly acquired series entitled *Your Future as a* ... As my eye scanned the nearly fifty volumes for careers that appealed to me, I was pleasantly surprised to discover a volume devoted to what I had theretofore considered an extremely esoteric profession: *Your Future as a Rabbi—A Calling that Counts* by Rabbi Alfred Gottschalk. I took the book from the shelf, sat down, and read it from cover to cover.

It may sound trite, but reading that book was a significant moment in the development of my vocational orientation. Before reading Rabbi Gottschalk's work, I had absolutely no idea what it took to become a rabbi. What did a future rabbi need to believe? What qualities did a future rabbi need to possess? What was the precise nature of rabbinic education? Why did "ordinary people" decide to study for the rabbinate?

I did not decide to become a rabbi right then and there. Yet, from reading *Your Future as a Rabbi*, I learned that my interests and abilities were appropriate for the rabbinate. Many of the questions first posed and then answered in the book were questions I myself had pondered when my own congregational rabbi suggested that I ought to consider becoming a rabbi. This book even provided answers to many of the questions I hesitated to ask out loud: Do all rabbis believe in God? Can one be a rabbi but not lead a congregation? I even learned that most rabbis earn an adequate income (despite my relatives' frequent suggestions that all rabbis were poor as "synagogue mice").

I could have hardly suspected that a mere fifteen years later I would not only be a rabbi, but the one primarily responsible for identifying, nurturing, and admitting students interested in the Rabbinic School at the Hebrew Union College–Jewish Institute of Religion. And more than that, the book's author —Rabbi Alfred Gottschalk—would be my *Rosh Yeshivah*, the distinguished President of the College–Institute!

In counseling hundreds of men and women who expressed interest in the rabbinate, I was delighted to learn that *Your Future as a Rabbi* was still being read by prospective rabbinic students nearly twenty years after its initial publication. Despite the fact that much of the specific information was dated, the book's overall approach still served its original purpose of providing students with the basic information they needed to contemplate a rabbinical career. In time, I realized that *Your Future as a Rabbi* continued to attract readers in spite of its age because the book was, in fact, sui generis; there still exists no comparable resource for aspiring rabbis.

Consequently, I am deeply grateful to Dr. Gottschalk for permitting me to revise this edition of his work. Let there be no mistake. The vast majority of this book remains unchanged from the first edition. I have simply endeavored to incorporate the many professional developments that have occurred since the book first appeared. Some of those changes, like the ordination of women, have profoundly affected the American rabbinate. Other revisions are essentially cosmetic in nature.

This new edition boasts one significant change: the addition of an extensive Bibliographic Essay on the American rabbinate since 1960. It is our hope that it will encourage aspiring rabbinic students to further reading and serve as a bibliographic direction for researchers and scholars.

In an eleventh-century Midrash we read the following incident:

A sage arrived from Laodicea. Rabbi Eleazar, Rabbi Simeon, and Rabbi Johanan ben Beroka came to visit the guest. He said to them: "It is my duty to thank you for preserving the Torah after I shall be gone. You also should thank your disciples for maintaining the Torah after you are gone. Moses was great, but if others had not kept the Torah after he had departed, of what use would his greatness have been?" (Midrash Lekah Tov on Deuteronomy, 32:46)

It is my hope that this new edition will contribute to the development of a new generation of rabbis and disciples who will carry the mantle of Torah into the twenty-first century.

Gary P. Zola
National Director of Admissions and Student Affairs
Hebrew Union College-Jewish Institute of Religion
Cincinnati, Ohio
June 1987
Erev Shavuot, 5747

Chapter I

Should I Be a Rabbi?

THE QUALITY OF JEWISH FAITH

Judaism as a religion and civilization represents one of the oldest and most vital philosophies of humankind. Parent faith to Christianity and Islam, it has nurtured a world view that teaches the great truth that God is One, and that a unity encompasses all people. Although these ideas are ancient, they are radical too, for much of the world is still torn by distrust, inequality, and a strident inhumanity. Amid ancient and modern barbarities, Judaism taught a doctrine of social justice and of the innate goodness of the human being. It championed each person as a being created in God's image, not as some hapless lackey to the forces of nature, to deities of stone, or to mortal despots who demanded craven obedience. When these ideas of human dignity were first conceived in the heartland of civilization—then known as Palestine—they shook the very foundations of society. Such thoughts were novel and represented a breakthrough in the development of the human conscience.

Because of Judaism's challenging and creative world outlook, it began to win spiritual adherents and in time leaped the confines of the narrow geographic borders in which it was reared to become a world religion of immense force. Christianity and Islam, which based themselves on biblical teachings, brought the insights of Judaism to the most benighted and obscure hamlets of the world. Great

1

centers of civilization also learned of Judaism for, in addition to the offshoots of the Jewish faith, Judaism itself remained vibrant and creative. From the destruction of the Second Temple by the Roman legions in the year 70 of this era, to the rebirth of the Jewish state in 1948, Jews settled in a vast Diaspora. No hub of intellectual, mercantile, or cultural activity was devoid of their presence. Wherever life was pulsating, there Jews brought their traditions and historic faith. Judaism, because it was a universal religion, was portable, and so Jews infused their environment with the religious truths that had first been revealed to them at Sinai and on the other great heights and deserts of the Holy Land. There, prophets saw visions of a world in which we need not "learn war anymore," humane priests taught the commandments of Moses, and sages probed the meaning of human existence.

Judaism remained an exciting faith because it successfully fought off the temptation to become preoccupied with otherworldliness. Certainly, the issues of an afterlife, immortality, and heaven and hell were studied and hotly debated. Basically, however, Judaism focused on the issues of the living. Its feet remained firmly planted on the ground. Judaism never lost its nerve or despaired of solving the problems of human existence in this world. That is why it retained its relevance even in the most tumultuous revolutions and intellectual upheavals.

That is also why contemporary America is so vitally interested in Jewish life and thought, and why so many books and plays on Jewish subjects are being written and widely read. The great interest in the Jew and in Judaism in America presents an interesting puzzle. Many sociological studies indicate that there is a shrinking difference in attitudes between American Jewry and the secular American culture in which it exists. And yet, precisely at this moment the American public is studying the Jews most intently. "In an age of 'alienation'," a *Time* magazine editorial opined, "the Jew is looked to as an expert in estrangement—the perpetual outsider who knows how to keep warm out there." But that is not all. The new spate of books depicting Jewish life also portrays a Jewish world view that is compelling. There is a tenacity in Judaism to bring light and truth to the world, often against incredible odds. In the cruel pangs of their recent suffering, Jews have maintained with Anne Frank–like simplicity that, despite all, people still have great capacity for goodness. How wistful such a hope must have seemed amid the Nazi atrocities. And yet hundreds of thousands of Jews went to their death with words of hope and prayer on their lips. "I believe with perfect faith," they chanted the old Maimonidean principle, ". . . that the Messiah will yet come. Though he may tarry, still I await him." How absurd these Jews must have seemed to their murderers and perhaps even to themselves. They hoped beyond the limits of hope in the individual's redemption from evil. But that is the Jew's eternal imperative: to be God's fool even in a world where Satan seems to hold sway. There is something schooled into the Jew by a faith that will not rest while the forces of destruction are loose in the world. Judaism instills a compulsion to work for the long-envisioned society, "Where each shall sit under the vine and under the fig tree and none shall be afraid." Perhaps it is this quality in the faith of Judaism that so captivates modern America, once again restless about its own dreams and ideals.

THE RELEVANCY OF THE RABBINIC CALLING

While the Jewish faith requires all of Israel to strive toward its espoused goals, there have always been those who, by virtue of leadership qualities, emerged to shape Judaism's destiny. Those who view Judaism predominantly as a religion have looked to a certain kind of leadership for guidance. For over two thousand years the Jewish people has relied upon its rabbis to be teachers par excellence of the Jewish tradition. The term *rabbi* means "my teacher" or "my master" and was used to designate one who was an accomplished scholar of Torah, both in its written and oral tradition, and who was ordained as such. Rabbinic accreditation was attested to by a certificate of ordination (*semikhah*), granted by an older scholar of unquestioned learning.[1] Since the formative period, in which the rabbinate evolved, its development has had several major phases. The rabbinate of today is permeated by the ideals of its historic prototypes, but new in style and character.

It must be made clear that the rabbinate is not a priesthood. While there are rabbis who are priests (*Kohanim*), many are not. By and large, rabbis come from the ranks of Jewish laity (*Yisrael*). The rites and ceremonies they perform are, from the Jewish legal aspect, permissible to any knowledgeable Israelite. Marriage ceremonies, funerals, baby namings, leading of public worship are the prerogatives of any learned Jew. The leader of public worship or ceremonial was the representative of the community before God. Rarely in tradition, except on stated occasions, did the rabbi of the community assume the role of precentor. Regrettably, the temper of modern times has greatly reduced the number of Jews who are sufficiently aware of the legal and ceremonial practices to perform these sacred rites themselves. Today, the rabbi's role is virtually that of religious official who performs all the functions previously accorded as a privilege to any worthy Jew. In a later chapter we shall see how this development came about, but suffice it to say that even in this new capacity the rabbi is not accorded the office of priest.

The rabbi is not an intermediary between God and the human. No Jew prays through a rabbi. The rabbi has no right to pardon sins or hear confession. The rabbi's views are

---

[1] Such was the procedure in Palestine in the period of the *Tannaim* (70–217 C.E. [Common Era]), the teachers of the Mishnah. In Babylonia those who taught the Mishnah, the authoritative law code compiled by Rabbi Judah the Prince (135–217 C.E.), were called *Amoraim*, expounders of the Mishnah. A teacher of the law ordained in that community was called *rav*, which also means "master" and "teacher." The title of an ordained Jewish scholar today follows the Palestinian designation.

his/her opinions, his/her considered judgments, or even verdicts based on his/her understanding of Jewish law; they are not indisputable dogma or a vehicle to heaven. Although significant differences exist among Orthodox (very traditional), Conservative, and Reform rabbis as to the nature of their calling, none would claim absolute authority in the interpretation of Torah. In American Jewish life the various enclaves of rabbis have developed platforms, guidelines, and norms of religious life, but these organizations have always been cognizant that the American Jew lives in a voluntaristic society. The American Jew may feel obliged to live under traditional discipline or orthodox Jewish law, but no Jew can be compelled to do so. In this environment of freedom, a premium has been put on the rabbi's ability to convince the modern Jew through sermons, lectures, and discussions. Religiosity cannot be coerced or commanded; it can only be induced through conviction maturing into firm belief.

The emancipation of the modern pulpit (especially in the United States) made the rabbinic calling into a potent force and was the end product of a hard and courageous struggle. The modern rabbi mentioned that Judaism had something to say about the rights of labor, about war and peace, about the growing alienation of the individual in a technological society. During the past several decades, Judaism has had some well-tested philosophies to apply to the mounting revolution in morals, to the problems of education and human relations. Questions were raised by an increasing number of Jewish college students on the compatibility of Judaism with science and with the insights of the new psychology discovered by Sigmund Freud. Rabbis followed the advice of the ingenious Ben Bag Bag of the Mishnah who advised, "Turn it [the Torah] and turn it over again, for everything is in it ..." Tradition and interpretation once again had to be expanded so that the new generation of Jews would not be "included out." The message of Judaism had once more to be brought into the marketplace of ideas and faiths that ventured forth to wrestle with the problems and perils of the modern world.

A generation of American rabbis dared to step outside of the conventional role of the rabbi as resource scholar expounding law and lore to a dwindling remnant of Talmud-trained Jews. The Hillel and the Jewish Chautauqua programs brought rabbis to the campuses. Jews and Christians began to confront one another as equals trying to understand each other's faith. Discussions that began at times with condescending tolerance developed into real dialogues, reversing two thousand years of intermittent animosity. The rabbi was in the forefront of these developments, often initiating bold new programs and approaches.

There were giants in the American rabbinate, for it was an age of expanding intellectual and moral frontiers. Individuals hewed out paths for Judaism where none existed before. Of Stephen S. Wise (1874–1949), one of the greatest of American rabbis of the past generation, the learned Rabbi Solomon Goldman (1893–1953) said, "Wises were born to rule Empires; all that Jewry could offer was a pulpit." Wise made much of his pulpit; he propelled it into the chancelleries of the world. Through him and others like him, Judaism with its dynamism, sense of justice, and restlessness with the "as is," once more spoke to the world. The modern rabbi, to paraphrase Ezekiel, sought that which was lost, brought back that which was driven away, bound up that which was broken, and strengthened that which was sick. The great legacy of the ancient rabbinate was given new coinage by bold courageous rabbis who sought to mold the modern Jew and world to the eternal ideals of Judaism.

It is the essence of tradition that worthwhile values and institutions be transmitted. That is why each year several hundred seminarians, newly ordained, enter the Jewish world to renew the traditions of the rabbinate and to leave their own impress upon it. As a teacher of rabbis, I have seen some outstanding young men and women, who in time will rise to the challenges of this era and bring the message of Judaism anew to this generation of Jews. Seminaries cannot mass-produce Stephen Wises, Abba Hillel Silvers, or Abraham

Joshua Heschels. They grow to maturity in novel circumstances and, in time, the new giants will rear their lionized heads and we will know that other great teachers of Judaism are on the horizon.

The intellectual and spiritual commitments required of the rabbi limit the available candidates for this calling. Yet it is my feeling that many young men and women of idealism and worth ask themselves the question, "Should I be a rabbi?" An individual who can rise to the great challenges of the rabbinate is not ordinary, and that is another reason why the fellowship of rabbis, be it Reform, Reconstructionist, Conservative, or Orthodox, is not large.

But what of those rabbinic candidates who enter the seminaries? What is their background and what motivates them? Many of the applicants to rabbinical seminaries decide to become rabbis because they have been inspired in their youth or on the college campus by some outstanding rabbinic personality. They seek to emulate someone whom they trust and for whom they have respect. Such candidates consider themselves disciples of a great teacher. There are other candidates whose initial impetus to enter the field came from other considerations. Orthodox young men, who were reared in *yeshivot* (all-day parochial schools) and whose total environment is Jewish, may have considered the rabbinate as the most logical extension of their intellectual training and religious pursuits. The rabbinate appears to this segment of candidates as the most natural environment for the enlargement of their Jewish learning, and for the opportunity to serve the segment of Jewish life that claims to be traditional or orthodox.

Still others enter the rabbinic academies because of personal experiences in religious camping. There are many encampments, sponsored by all religious groups, whose programs focus upon providing an intensive and wholesome environment in which Judaism is lived naturally and daily. This encounter has a transforming effect on a young person; life values often fall into place and Judaism's message to the world becomes a passionate concern. From this experience also, the rabbinate may seem a clear choice that will make it possible to devote oneself to a lifetime of service.

Yet another clear category of rabbinical student is more frequently found in the Reform and Conservative seminaries. This is a core of hard-thinking young people who may or may not have come from a religious environment; or, having come from one, have broken discipline with it to seek their own way in the world. They may be fervent Zionists or non-Zionists, mystical or rational by temperament. The *meaning* of Judaism marks their quest. They look to their ancestral faith as one that needs to address itself to the burning issues of our time; it must have the bite of relevance. In their view, tradition cannot be produced to attest to its own validity. Existence and reason, as well as tradition, represent the criteria for the evaluation of Jewish belief, custom, and ceremony. Such candidates often evince a hunger for knowledge and constitute a great challenge to the seminaries. It is not uncommon for such highly motivated students to reach the very top of their class by the time of ordination.

Amid the great diversity of backgrounds that the candidates bring with them are some vital and irreducible common denominators. While a student's God-concept may not yet be fixed, he or she acknowledges by thoughts and deeds the presence of divine power in this life. God is a reality about which one thinks as well as to whom one prays. Performance of *mitzvot* (acts originating from religious commitment) represents the true inner being. They may range from wearing *tefilin* (phylacteries) to participating in a civil rights or peace march. Theological problems of all sorts should be of interest. A theological student in a Jewish seminary must master a vast intellectual tradition in which difference of viewpoint is abundantly evident. The student must be prepared to stretch his or her mind to understand the issues involved and must evidence a passion for the pursuit of truth. Looming as perhaps the most immediately relevant common denominator is the student's involvement with the destiny of the Jewish people. The tangible expression of the success or failure of Judaism manifests itself in the concept of Jewish peoplehood. The survival of Judaism through Jews must genuinely engage every waking moment. And in sleep, the rabbi must dare to dream this people's timeless vision of a just and peaceful world, in which the program of Judaism has been expanded to worldwide dimensions.

There is room in the rabbinic fellowship for young men and women for whom these concerns are vital and who would make them the occupation of their daily life. The rabbinate can be one of the most useful, creative, and satisfying careers. There is no end of good work and programming that can be done. And today, there is *no dearth* of pulpits or of educational or institutional opportunities requiring spiritual leadership.

CAREER OPPORTUNITIES

The modern rabbinate is composed of persons who have been ordained in Orthodox, Conservative, Reconstructionist, or Reform seminaries. There are rabbis in America who are graduates of great European *yeshivot* and seminaries. There are also those (mostly Orthodox in affiliation) who hold private ordination. To become eligible for ordination as a rabbi, a candidate must complete a course of study that varies in length depending upon one's previous knowledge and the requirements of the seminary in question. All of the branches of Judaism stress certain theological emphases, and one may properly expect these to be reflected in the curricula of the seminaries they sponsor.

Great similarities of vocational opportunity hold true for any ordained rabbi, irrespective of the seminary from which ordination was received. The largest number of rabbis actively engaged in full-time rabbinic work is found in congregational situations. Because of the growing number of Jewish families affiliated with congregations, senior rabbis often engage recent graduates to be their assistants. A good assistantship affords the younger colleague great opportunity to learn the intricacies of the profession from a seasoned senior. Many assistants supervise the religious school and share pastoral and sermonic duties. Assistant positions may grow into associate posts if the opportunity is present and the colleagues find themselves compatible.

Increasingly, other opportunities are available for rabbis in religiously oriented institutions. The major branches of Judaism have national congregational organizations. In the Reform movement, for example, the Union of American Hebrew Congregations (UAHC) engages rabbis as regional directors for its various councils. In addition, rabbis direct national education, youth, camping, religious action, interfaith, and synagogal activities. The Orthodox, Conservative, and Reconstructionist movements afford similar opportunities for administrative positions. Hillel Foundations engage great numbers of rabbis to direct the programs of Jewish youth on university campuses throughout the United States and Canada. In some instances, a Hillel directorship carries with it the opportunity to teach Judaica on the campus. At the same time, growing numbers of seminary and university teaching opportunities are developing. Full-time chairs in Jewish studies and in Hebrew language and literature are being established at a rate that continues to dramatize the lack of qualified candidates to occupy them. To fill these vacancies, university administrators are regularly turning to scholarly rabbis.

Because education makes the rabbi an expert in Jewish lore, many Jewish communal organizations engage rabbis as executive directors. Bureaus of Jewish Education, the B'nai B'rith, the American Jewish Committee, the American Jewish Congress, the National Jewish Welfare Board, and the National Conference of Christians and Jews all have at one time or another employed rabbi-administrators. The various Zionist organizations and youth and camping institutes constantly seek rabbis in a professional capacity to carry out their programs. The military chaplaincy has become the lifework of a number of rabbis, as has the institutional chaplaincy. In the latter instance, rabbis are engaged, usually through the National Jewish Welfare Board, to serve as spiritual leaders and counselors to patients in hospitals of all kinds, in orphanages, prisons, and homes for the aged. At present, a striking number of rabbinic opportunities exists abroad. Congregations in New Zealand, Australia, South Africa, South America, Great Britain, Europe, and Israel are eagerly seeking candidates to fill pulpits and administrative positions in Jewish communal agencies.

By far the greatest number of pulpit vacancies exists in the United States itself. Scores of congregations lack professional religious leadership. Because candidates for pulpits cluster in and about metropolitan centers with large Jewish populations, smaller communities often go unserved. If they are fortunate in securing the services of a theological student in training, their need is somewhat lessened. The number of students now graduating from the major seminaries is *clearly inadequate* to meet the growing needs of the synagogues, temples, and service agencies. At no period in Jewish history has the time been more opportune to increase the "disciples of the wise" so that Judaism may be more nobly served.

THE STATUS OF THE PROFESSION

In 1954 the American Jewish community concluded its tercentenary celebration. The occasion elicited many studies of American Jewry. Among projects undertaken was a study by the Jewish Statistical Bureau under the direction of H. S. Linfield on "The Rabbis of the United States." The study examined (1) the number of rabbis in the United States —Orthodox, Conservative, and Reform; (2) rabbinical training; (3) secular education; and (4) areas of service.

The study indicated that in the first two centuries of Jewish history in the United States, beginning in 1654, the growth in the number of rabbis was relatively moderate. This situation changed drastically during the second half of the nineteenth century so that by 1900, 526 rabbis were listed in the Jewish Directory. In 1954 the *Registry of American Rabbis* contained 4,257 names. The number of rabbis has continued to increase so that in 1986 nearly 1,500 rabbis were affiliated with the association of Reform Rabbis, known as the Central Conference of American Rabbis (CCAR); 1,200 rabbis, with the association of Conservative rabbis, the Rabbinical Assembly of America (RA); and 2,100 rabbis, with three associations of Orthodox rabbis: the Union of Orthodox Rabbis of the United States and Canada, the Rabbinical Council of America (RCA), and the Rabbinical Alliance of America (*Igud Ha-Rabonim*). This grouping indicates that 4,600 rabbis are currently affiliated with the major national associations of rabbis.

Historically speaking, the Central Conference of American Rabbis is the oldest of the rabbinic associations, created in 1889 by Isaac Mayer Wise. The Rabbinical Assembly of America was formed in 1901; the Union of Orthodox Rabbis of the United States and Canada, in 1902; the Rabbinical Council of America, 1923; the Rabbinical Alliance of America, 1944. The standards of these associations admit to membership only men and women (in the CCAR and RA only) who are ordained by recognized seminaries and authorities, and who comport themselves with the highest standards of the profession.

Other associations of rabbis are smaller in number and influence and do not have uniform professional standards for admission. Moreover, some rabbis involved in congregational or allied fields are not members of the major national associations. Of these unaffiliated rabbis, many were trained and ordained abroad. Another group of unaffiliated rabbis consists of persons currently engaged in other occupations.

Making allowances for reasonable growth in the national rabbinic organizations, one may estimate that today there are 6,500 rabbis in the United States, of whom the Orthodox are still most numerous and the Conservative and Reform have remained relatively equal in number.

The salaries of rabbis are dependent upon many factors. Beginning salaries are certainly comparable with other professional starting salaries (such as law or accounting). Of course, some rabbis begin at lower salaries and others at higher. Generally, rabbinic salaries provide a rabbi with a very comfortable life-style. The usual salary of a rabbi in the field for ten years varies in relation to the size and affluence of the community. Usually, smaller congregations cannot provide their rabbis with as high a salary as larger ones. However, opportunities of the latter category are limited and are usually won by the most prominent persons in the profession. On the other hand, many important rabbis elect to remain in smaller congregations and at smaller salary scales because they are convinced that they can render a more valuable service in such an environment. Rabbis may also augment their income by emoluments for officiating at ceremonies such as weddings and funerals. However, many rabbis donate such emoluments to the temple or to a charitable fund within the temple that is distributed at the rabbi's discretion.

Salary schedules for rabbis who specialize in Jewish community service are difficult to obtain, since they vary so much with the particular agency. More often than not, where responsibilities are comparable, salaries are competitive with those paid by congregations. Included in this category are the chaplaincy, both military and nonmilitary, the field of Jewish education, and Jewish social and welfare work.

As in every profession, there are those who for a period of time are unemployed. The reasons may vary from problems of professional competence to temporary illness. Retired rabbis have become a more prominent group in recent years as well.

PAST AND PRESENT—THE CHANGING ROLE OF THE RABBI

It is still true, other opportunities notwithstanding, that most rabbinic students hope to become congregational rabbis. Whether the candidate be Orthodox, Conservative, or Reform, the pulpit represents the historical medium for imparting the teachings of Judaism. There has been, of late, considerable discussion on the changing role of the rabbi. Articles and essays have appeared in popular and learned journals attempting to define precisely what it is that the congregational rabbi of today is expected to do to perform both the historic function of teacher of Judaism and the role of minister to an evergrowing following of synagogue-affiliated Jews. Much of this discussion reflects the growing pains of an ancient calling trying to adapt to the climate of modern life and to the new needs of burgeoning communities. Rabbi Norman Hirsh of Seattle, Washington, preached a sermon to his congregation entitled, "What Is a Rabbi?" and made the following observations:

I can think of fourteen important tasks I perform:

Visiting the sick
Counseling the troubled
Conducting services
Preaching
Supervising the religious school
Teaching children, both confirmation class and bar
    mitzvah students
Adult education
Officiating at weddings, funerals, etc.
Interfaith speaking in the community
Temple administration
Building a temple or worrying about new facilities
Temple programming, including the bulletin
Teaching converts

The number of tasks the rabbi performs is staggering. And without wisdom and determination, the ability to say no as well as yes, the rabbi will be totally fragmented.

I am not essentially an administrator, a builder of temples, a counselor, an ambassador to the non-Jews, or any of the dozen other functions I perform. I am a rabbi, a Jew trained in scholarship, and my central task is to learn and to teach.

It is unquestionably the temper of modern times that has created the condition in which rabbis and congregants ask themselves the question that is the title of Rabbi Hirsh's sermon, "What *is* a rabbi?"

To carry the discussion further, it would be helpful to look at some historic facts on the origin and development of the rabbinate. As has been said, the history of rabbinic ordination goes back to the first centuries of our era. Particularly after the destruction of the Second Temple in 70 C.E. was it necessary to determine upon whom the mantle of leadership should lie. It fell upon a remarkable group of rabbis deeply learned in the law, whose credential was their *semikhah*, or ordination. These rabbis played such a vital part in the perpetuation and enlargement of Judaism that in the second century of the Common Era, when the Emperor Hadrian sought to destroy this ancient faith, he prohibited the ordination of rabbis. The penalty for the ordainer and the ordained, if discovered, was death. The city in which the ordination took place was to be put to the sword.

Jewish history records that many of the great rabbis, as well as their students, jeopardized their lives to maintain the practice of ordination because it had come to mean the lawful transfer of authority from one generation of scholars to the next. For example, the aged Judah ben Baba gathered five disciples in a secluded spot between the cities of Usha and Shefaram to ordain them. The group was betrayed by informers, and Roman soldiers soon closed in. Before the legionnaires arrived, ben Baba ordained the disciples, who barely escaped capture. Their great teacher, however, was caught and, according to the Talmud, Roman soldiers drove three hundred javelins into his body. Judah, fully aware that discovery meant certain death, elected nevertheless to sacrifice his life so that Torah might endure.

Before the creation of the rabbinate as an institution, three leadership types were clearly delineated in the Bible. The book of Jeremiah states, "For instruction shall not perish from the priest, nor counsel from the wise, nor the word from the prophet." In the rabbinate these three functions of

Jewish leadership were integrated and thereby perpetuated. It was Thomas Carlyle who proclaimed in his *Heroes and Hero Worship* that "universal history, the history of what man has accomplished in this world, is at the bottom the history of the great men who have worked here." This is certainly true of the architects of Judaism, the priests, prophets, and sages who prepared the mind-set of the Jewish people so that it might become a bearer of truth to the world.

The prophet was a dynamic leader who represented no societal institution nor vested interest, but truth as his mind and heart understood it. The prophets believed that their message emanated from divine inspiration and from a confrontation with God. The Hebrew prophet addressed himself to the question of what it was that God desired of the individual in human society. One of them answered in the sublime language, "Only to do justice, to love mercy, and to walk humbly with thy God." The Hebrew prophets emerge as God-intoxicated men and women who gave leadership to their people by their understanding of religious obligation, manifest in the conduct of their own lives. This sort of dynamic leader sprang from no particular caste. Aristocracy of birth was not a prerequisite for this mission. Prophets enjoyed no special privileges in society. To the contrary, often they suffered penalties for the uncompromising way in which they spoke the truth.

The priesthood was another category of leadership, perhaps best designated as "symbolic leadership." Priests fulfilled their duties often as official representatives at the local or national shrines. "Torah" represents the priest's concern. The priest was an expert in ritual matters who knew the distinction between the holy and the profane. The priest showed concern for order, legalism, and religious conduct. The writer Ahad Ha-Am (Asher Ginsberg, 1856–1927), in an essay entitled "Priest and Prophet," brilliantly pointed out the additional function of the priesthood in early Hebrew culture. Charged with the task of translating prophetic ideals into the fabric of society, the priest often acted as mediator between the status quo and the new idea whose time had come.

The sage was yet another type of teacher, the wise leader from whom counsel was sought. Unlike the prophet and the priest, the sage approached the problems of the world in pragmatic terms, perceiving the dynamic in human relationships and then projecting modes of conduct in harmony with the law of God and the law of the universe.

The rabbis synthesized these three qualities of leadership and created a powerful composite, able to respond to the needs of their time. The rabbis were a scholar class who belonged to a movement within Judaism known as the Pharisees. In the opinion of Rabbi Leo Baeck (1873–1956), the Pharisees comprised "the people's party." The rabbis waged a relentless battle for the status of the individual Jew. To this Jew, the rabbis offered a deed-oriented religion, which also imposed learning as an obligation of Jewish heritage. This approach enabled the Pharisees to create a revolutionary religious, social, and educational institution called the synagogue, whose threefold purpose as a house of assembly (*Bet Knesset*), a house of prayer (*Bet Tefillah*), and a house of study (*Bet Midrash*) survives to this day.

A Pharisaic sage was called a *Talmid Hakham*. The Jew looked to this sage with confidence for interpretations relating to educational, spiritual, and legal matters. The *Talmid Hakham* was an authority figure, not only because he was learned in Judaic matters but because he was a rounded scholar, a man of the world, able to concern himself with secular as well as religious matters. In the period of the Tannaim (70–217 C.E.), ordained *Talmide Hakhamim* were not compensated because of their title of rabbi. All the talmudic sages earned their livelihood through some other occupation. The rabbis of this period were conscious of the teaching, "Make not of the Torah a crown wherewith to aggrandize yourself, nor a spade with which to dig." The sage Hillel was a woodchopper; Shammai, a builder; Joshua ben Hananiah, a blacksmith; Akiba, a shepherd; Johanan, a cobbler. Still others were tailors, water carriers, linguists, poets, astronomers, or students of natural history. Some were physicians, and others farmers and merchants. During the talmudic period the chief interest of the rabbis was the *halakhah* (law). Their *semikhah* was a judicial degree that conferred special status upon the rabbi who was concerned with the teaching and adjudication of the law. There were also those whose ordination designated them as preachers and teachers of the *agadah*, the nonlegal portions of the Talmud. The sermon was a regular part of the Sabbath morning service in the talmudic period, where *agadah* was used for the purpose of public instruction.

By the middle of the fourteenth century, the tradition of not receiving compensation for rabbinic services underwent a radical change. After the terrible plague of the Black Death, the scholars who survived the catastrophe, and who lacked capital, found themselves compelled to make the teaching of the Torah the means of their livelihood. Beginning with the fifteenth century, the rabbinate gradually became a profession. With rabbinic irony, and cognizant of the ancient teaching that one should not be compensated for teaching Torah, the rabbi's salary was defined as *sekhar battalah*, compensation for being prevented from engaging in a gainful occupation. Rabbinic emoluments, however, were minimal, and many rabbis maintained themselves through additional occupations, stipends from communal taxes, and fees received for sitting as judges. It was also the rabbi's responsibility to maintain an academy, to teach in it, and to examine the students.

The rabbi was required to set an example of devotion to study. It was not unusual for the rabbi to spend most waking hours poring over the intricate legal codes and other rabbinic literature in order to respond to questions of law on the basis of precedents established in that literature. If he—and all rabbis were men during this period—was quite expert, other communities would consult him in writing on questions of law, to which he would respond. This body of legal material, known as the Responsa Literature, contains case law that he had to know to fulfill his function as judge and arbiter. The rabbi also became the molder of communal institutions and the guardian of moral conduct. It was his obligation to motivate people to acts of charity and to support the welfare institutions created. The rabbi would preach on special occasions and was accorded the honor of reading services on certain holidays. These enormous responsibilities of the rabbi could be met only through devotion and, at times, through great personal sacrifice.

The ghetto presented another distinct chapter in the development of the rabbinate. Originally, the ghetto came into being in the late Middle Ages when Jews, through legal enactments, were segregated in certain areas of cities and towns. The ghetto was established in Germany after the Black Death in 1348–1349 and in Venice in 1516. It created an isolationist type of Judaism, which, nevertheless, enabled the Jew to survive this critical period of his history. While Judaism was never monolithic in ideology, it always contained a vast central core of law and tradition to which Jews subscribed. In the ghetto, conformity to that tradition was mandatory. In the ghetto there was self-government, which commanded the allegiance of those who dwelt within its walls. Although the ghetto created inner cohesiveness and loyalty to the Jewish group, it remained intellectually sealed off from the rest of the world. There emerged in the ghetto the *Rav*, who usually was as impressive in appearance as in his learning. It was his task to act as judge in lawsuits and to answer questions of ritual. On two occasions during the year he delivered sermons. The *Rav* became the symbol of Jewish piety and learning and was greatly revered for those qualities. In Eastern Europe, until the dawn of the twentieth century and in some communities to this very day, the *Rav* represents the embodiment of authority in matters pertaining to Jewish tradition.

Moses Mendelssohn (1729–1786), the father of the Jewish Enlightenment in Germany, sought to bring an end to ghetto-type isolation. Mendelssohn said that Judaism could survive in the modern world only if it became a religious persuasion whose truths were rational and universal. In his book *Jerusalem* (1783), Mendelssohn developed an approach for the separation of church and state. The state, he reasoned, may not legislate what an individual must believe; it cannot regulate the ideas or the convictions of its citizens. Conversely, religion must be shorn of all political power; its force must be moral, influencing the state by instruction and persuasion. It was Mendelssohn's theory to separate the powers of church and state so that religion could flourish freely without external coercion.

Until the time of the French Revolution, the conditions outside the ghetto held no temptations for intellectual or social exploration. This state of affairs changed drastically when Napoleon Bonaparte demolished the ghettos on his march to conquest. The French Revolution and the ideals it held out of "liberty, equality and fraternity" created a most attractive world of which to be a part. At least that is what was thought by the most gifted and ambitious members of the community who were daring to reach out into the larger world. In 1807, attempting to consolidate the gains of the revolution, Napoleon convened a high court, which was called the Sanhedrin. He patterned it after the Great Palestinian Sanhedrin of antiquity, so that its authority would be unquestioned by the newly emancipated Jews. His purpose in calling the Jewish notables together was to get the sanction of the organized Jewish community for his plan of stripping all religions of their power to adjudicate civil law. Napoleon wanted religion removed from politics, and the Sanhedrin he called agreed to his terms on behalf of the Jewish communities under his rule.

The rabbis who had judged matters that were now to be tried by the civil courts lost considerable authority over their coreligionists. No longer could Jewish affairs be decided solely according to *halakhah*, particularly in the domain of personal status, e.g., laws of marriage, divorce, and inheritance. Whereas previously it was impossible for a Jew to be married outside the authority of *halakhah*, now a civil magistrate could be approached if one so desired. The state, in effect, protected the newly emancipated Jew from *halakhah* so that a person could, if he or she chose, be severed completely from the religious community.

Mendelssohn's theory and Bonaparte's politics conspired

to denude Judaism of all of its national qualities and beliefs and made it into a religion, a persuasion. This was the price of emancipation and of citizenship. The formula that evolved in Germany and France became also the formula for religious life in America. In fact, it is only in America that some significant form of separation of church and state truly exists. Nowhere in the world does religious pluralism flourish as here, and nowhere in the world is Mendelssohn's plea for the separation of church and state more cherished.

The far-reaching philosophical premises advocated by Mendelssohn and the practical enforcement of those ideas for other reasons by Bonaparte could not fail to throw the traditional rabbinate into turmoil. The question of what the rabbinate was to become arose at this juncture in history, and it is a question that is still being posed today. The Orthodox rabbinate, which has never made peace with the separation of powers, has held on to every conceivable thread of *halakhic* authority. For the Orthodox, all *halakhah* is divinely revealed law. To surrender *halakhah*, even in civil matters, is grudgingly done. For example, no divorced Orthodox person may marry another Orthodox person unless a religious, as well as a civil, divorce has been secured. The argument runs that since marriage is a sacrament sealed by *halakhah*, it cannot be abrogated except through *halakhah*. The Conservative rabbinate has of late developed a similar position on the principles involved in such a question. The Reform rabbinate broke in principle with the binding authority of *halakhah*; it looks to civil authority to adjudicate questions arising out of the laws of personal status.

It was inevitable that in Europe, under these pressures, a new kind of rabbinate emerged. Rabbinic schools had to be created to train rabbis who could preserve Judaism in the modern world. In 1829, in Padua, a rabbinic college was opened in which, by royal decree, candidates for the rabbinate needed a doctorate in philosophy. It was in Germany, however, upon the urging of the great Reform Rabbi Abraham Geiger (1810–1874), that a plan was developed for the creation of a Jewish theological faculty to be affiliated with a German university. Geiger felt that a seminary should be located in the heart of the intellectual life of the times, not be isolated and exclusive. Geiger's plan for a liberal seminary did not immediately pan out. The first seminary was established in Breslau, in 1854, and was representative of what we call Conservative Judaism. Its director was the great scholar Zacharias Frankel (1801–1875), who opposed radical reform as well as ultra-Orthodoxy. The curriculum of the seminary was comprehensive, and the subjects were taught with scientific thoroughness.

In 1869, Geiger and Ludwig Philippson (1811–1889) once again pleaded for the creation of a Jewish theological faculty, where men of different religious viewpoints would occupy the important chairs. It was proposed that there should be full freedom in academic research and in the presentation of Jewish thought. It was also argued that no conformity of religious practice be required of the students. The major emphasis was on Jewish knowledge and its academic pursuit. The seminary opened in 1872 and shaped the thought of Reform Judaism. It was called the *Hochschule fuer die Wissenschaft des Judentums* (Institute for the Academic Study of Judaism).

In 1873, Dr. Israel Hildesheimer (1820–1899) of Berlin established the Orthodox rabbinical seminary that became, in a sense, a prototype for the Isaac Elchanan Yeshivah of New York, as Breslau had been for the Jewish Theological Seminary of America, and the *Hochschule* for the Hebrew Union College. It was on American soil, particularly after the decimation of the European Jewish communities in World War II, that the ideologies of modern Judaism came to maturity.

It is evident that the nucleus of the role of the modern rabbi was present throughout the various phases of the development of the rabbinate as an institution. In the modern world, to all of the traditional functions of the rabbi had to be added the function of relating Jewish life and institutions to the rigors of the scientific age.

The present-day emphases of the rabbinate in America grew out of the principle of voluntarism in religious association. On these shores, a unique type of Jewish communal life developed. Autonomous Jewish congregations emerged in all branches of Judaism. Each congregation reserved for itself the right and the privilege of electing its own rabbi. From the ultra-Orthodox to the most Reform, this freedom is still cherished today. There are presently voluntary congregational organizations such as the United Synagogue, the Union of American Hebrew Congregations, and the Union of Orthodox Jewish Congregations of America, as well as national placement commissions for each of these congregational units. Normally, rabbis select congregations whose pattern of religious practice is closest to their own viewpoint. It is not uncommon, however, to find that rabbis whose ideology was initially mismatched with that of their congregation are able over the years to weld their viewpoint and that of the congregation closer together.

The modern congregation that emerged in America demanded a religious program that would update Judaism and enable the Jew to live as an emancipated Jew in an open society. As in past history, it inevitably fell to the rabbi to develop a viable Jewish life within such an environment. Modern congregations tend to be self-sufficient; they have their own religious schools, halls of worship, and social and religious programs and often host events such as interfaith services that are of communal importance. Most congregations have men's clubs and women's clubs, parent-teacher associations, young people's leagues, senior citizen programs, adult study lectures and seminars, and, of course, a full cycle of religious activity. Membership in such congregations is normally requisite for participation in many or all of these activities. Every congregation, however, provides for families who are interested in its program but are unable to meet the financial obligations attendant on normal membership.

Members of a congregation normally elect their board, and either the congregation as a whole or the board then elects the rabbi. Serving a congregation with many internal organizations and programmatic needs is not an easy task. It is a constant challenge to the rabbi and those who are associated with him or her: an assistant, if the congregation is large, the cantor, the principal of the school, the executive director, and the boards and committees of the congregation. All must work together as a team to carry out the avowed program of a particular temple.

It is evident that the rabbi must be the spiritual force giving direction to the various facets of Jewish congregational life if it is to be permeated with the ideals of Judaism. This often puts the rabbi on a hectic treadmill of activities, but there is hardly a profession in the world that demands so much of an individual and, in turn, gives back so much in deep satisfaction. That is not to say that the rabbi is free of frustration. Because the rabbi wants to do so much and finds that the wheels of progress grind so exceedingly slowly, the aims that are held clearly in mind tend to be long delayed in accomplishment. It has become part of the rabbi's duty to teach and convince others of the rightness of his or her position, and this is an inevitable part of the rabbi's work.

The rabbis, who have always been the avant-garde of Judaism and the molders of tradition according to the needs of the time, are logically the first ones exposed to the winds of change. As Jewish life undergoes transformations, so does the rabbinate. To the question, "What is a rabbi?" it might then be proper to answer that he or she is a virtuoso of Judaism, whose artistry requires playing heavily on one string of faith while pressing lightly on the others until the proper melody emerges—harmonious and fitting. Themes that were major in one generation become minor in another, and new themes have yet to be created. It is for this role that the rabbi has been chosen by the instrumentalities of Jewish history and Jewish destiny. It is to these two, then, that a rabbi must expertly respond.

THE RABBI AS A TEACHER OF JUDAISM: PRIEST, PROPHET, OR SAGE?

The late Rabbi Jacob Shankman (1904–1986) observed in a fascinating essay, "The Changing Role of the Rabbi," that the inevitable substratum of the rabbinate is scholarship and teaching. Rabbi Shankman noted that the modern rabbi must at least be "a Jewish book-man familiar with the rich treasures of contemporary scholarly research and even aspire to make one specific area of study and learning his own." It is not uncommon to find in the rabbinate those who have specialized in philosophy, psychology, sociology, family counseling, and a host of other intellectual and vocational interests, all of which they seek to integrate into their traditional calling and learning. Because of the nature of American religious life, the rabbi not only teaches his or her congregation but often is invited to speak to other groups about Judaism. The rabbi accepts invitations to address Christian congregations and to lecture on campuses throughout the United States to Jewish and non-Jewish college students. It is often necessary to present an intellectual exposition of Judaism to the Christian clergy, which is eager to know of the antecedents of Christianity and views the rabbi as expert in that area.

While the subject matter that the contemporary American rabbi must attempt to translate into a meaningful reality is different from that of the medieval and ancient counterpart, we can see that the function of the institution of the rabbinate remains the same. It has as its primary obligation the teaching and interpretation of Judaism to Jews and to the world. It continues to be a hard but creative struggle. Judaism champions the quest rather than the pat answer to the complex problems of life and knowledge.

The rabbi, who is expected to be a pastor and counselor to the congregation, must know something of psychology and of group dynamics. As early as 1890, at the first annual convention of the Central Conference of American Rabbis in Cleveland, a rabbi saw as a new feature of the modern rabbinate the need to visit one's congregants in an attempt to get to know them and their personal needs. It was not without a struggle that the rabbis accepted this particular function of the rabbinate. In recent years it has grown to almost unmanageable proportions and has resulted, as Rabbi Robert Gordis has observed, in a sort of topsy-turvy reversal of the rabbinic roles. ''Instead of the rabbi being the scholar and the teacher par excellence, with few peripheral functions, scholarship became secondary, or less than that, and peripheral functions became central, and these in turn proliferated into a vast complex of activities.''

It soon became apparent that the field of counseling required as much expertise in its own way as had the exposition of Jewish lore in a previous period. As more and more people brought their personal (as opposed to legal) problems to their spiritual leader, the rabbi felt obliged to be conversant with community resources to which troubled people might turn for help. The rabbi became, and is, more of a specialist in referral than a psychotherapist or psychiatric social worker. Although a number of rabbis have specialized and earned their doctorates in this field, their pulpit work and their other congregational obligations prevent them from becoming full-time counselors within the congregation. Given the fact that the congregant turns to the rabbi, this function of the modern rabbinate is emerging as a matter of concern. The rabbi must know something about the nature of modern psychiatric techniques and therapies.

The modern rabbi is frequently called upon to be an organizer and administrator. In the 1930s the largest congregations in America had memberships of 500 to 800 families, with very few over 1,000. In 1986 dozens of congregations exceed 1,200 families, and some exceed 2,500. Of course, the rabbis of such congregations usually have one or more assistants. The larger the congregation, the greater are the administrative and organizational problems, to say nothing of the great demands made upon the rabbi's time for pastoral counseling, teaching, and lecturing. No matter how determined the rabbi may be to avoid administrative and organizational problems, the modern rabbinate necessitates the rabbi's involvement in decision-making previously unknown to the profession. For example, the rabbi must have some understanding of how a budget is created and administered; the rabbi must be zealous of the allocations for his or her religious program and constantly alert to the danger of proliferation of activity extraneous to the religious program of the congregation.

The increasing number of vital communal needs, both local and national, also concerns the rabbi. There is hardly a worthy cause in the United States, and in many instances abroad, that does not seek the rabbi's attention and support. These may range from human rights to the establishment of children's villages in Israel, from the rescuing of Jews in countries where Jewish existence is hazardous to a new *mikveh* (ritual bath) that some rabbi wishes to build. The rabbi must choose, from among the many demands, those that are paramount in importance.

The rabbi is expected to be involved, and can be particularly potent, in local causes. The boards of the hospitals, symphony, museum, public library, and even colleges and universities may turn to the rabbi for assistance. Because these causes are worthwhile and members of the congregation benefit from them, the rabbi must seek to strengthen the social and cultural institutions that uplift community life. For similar reasons, the rabbi may find it necessary to speak out prophetically against local, national, and international conditions that betray human inequality and are injurious to the perpetuation of Judaism and of the Jewish people. The rabbi is expected to take an interest in developments in the State of Israel, particularly as they affect Jewry in America and the rest of the world. Far from being a marriage and burial clerk, a master of ceremonies, or a joiner, the rabbi represents a positive social and communal force and is a central figure in the Jewish community.

As American Jewry continues to move forward, the rabbinate will gain even greater significance. To meet these new challenges, the rabbi would do well to remain true to his or her calling: a perpetual student of Judaism but at home in the intellectual climate of the modern world. By integrating in his or her person the ancient roles of sage, priest, and prophet, the rabbi should develop individual gifts as preacher, teacher, and counselor to convey a message forcefully and honestly. Amid complex duties and responsibilities, the rabbi faces moments of truth, realizing that one person cannot do everything equally well. A rabbi therefore sharpens the tool of his or her rabbinate in specific functions, be it preaching, teaching, counseling, or communal work, and learns to do those phases of rabbinic work with great expertise and resourcefulness. Any young man or woman with the prerequisite verbal and intellectual gifts, who possesses a deep love for the Jewish people and its religious tradition, can become a rabbi.

WOMEN IN THE RABBINATE

The advent of women rabbis is unquestionably the most dramatic and far-reaching development that has occurred in the American rabbinate since the first edition of this book appeared in 1967. In a short section of the book, I attempted to address the then timely question "Should a woman be a rabbi?" I argued that women would undoubtedly enter the rabbinate one day. Yet I hardly suspected that the historic opportunity and sacred duty to ordain the first woman rabbi, Sally Priesand, would fall upon me only a short time later. The ordination of Rabbi Priesand at HUC-JIR in 1972 was for me a turning point in my own rabbinate. I shall never forget the emotion-laden moment when Sally's classmates stood in thunderous ovation as the first woman rabbi descended from the pulpit of the Isaac M. Wise Plum Street Temple in Cincinnati after her ordination.

In reviewing the words I wrote in this book a mere twenty years ago, I delight in my prophetic falterings. I wrote: "... the Reform movement seems to be the only available vehicle to a young woman who wishes to qualify for ordination as a rabbi." Although the Hebrew Union College–Jewish Institute of Religion was indeed the first American seminary to ordain women rabbis, the Reconstructionist Rabbinical College (established in 1968) followed suit only a few years later. In 1983 the faculty of the Jewish Theological Seminary voted to admit women to its rabbinic school, and in 1985 Amy Eilberg became the first Conservative woman rabbi in

America. Thus, three of the four major rabbinical seminaries in the United States have undertaken to ordain women rabbis; more than 140 women rabbis had been ordained in American seminaries by 1986.

Indeed, it is mind-boggling to contemplate the dramatic upsurge of women rabbis that has occurred over the past fifteen years. We have hardly begun to comprehend how this vital development will affect the character of Jewish life in America. In time, half of all non-Orthodox rabbis will be women; most American Jews will sometime in their lives be served by female spiritual leaders. This undeniable fact will change forever the face of Jewish life in America—and the world.

Today, women have entered all kinds of rabbinic endeavors. A significant proportion of women rabbis work in congregational positions, and many others serve as Hillel directors or institutional officers. Several women occupy their own pulpits. Some congregations may still be unaccustomed to the presence of women in the rabbinate, but I believe women will undoubtedly soon come to occupy the larger, prestigious pulpits as the number with senior status (those in the rabbinate for more than ten years) increases.

In spite of the numerous challenges facing women who are attempting to forge a career in a profession so firmly rooted in masculine association, many women rabbis would concur with Rabbi Marla Feldman, who recently said:

> Actually, I have found that [being a woman] has worked to my advantage more often than to my disadvantage, and that more people—once they get over their initial shock, if they have shock—are willing to look at me as a person, and if they see me as someone with integrity and good intentions, then they no longer see me as a "woman rabbi."

Women entering the American rabbinate today will benefit from several support organizations founded by trail-blazing colleagues to assist them in assuming their rabbinic roles. The

Women's Rabbinic Network (WRN) is a national organization consisting of mostly Reform women rabbis. The WRN meets annually and serves as an important forum for professional development and colleagueship among women in the rabbinate.

Young men and women reading these words in the final decade of the twentieth century will have benefited from the first generation of women rabbis who capably served as models for all who care to follow. Thanks to a handful of pioneers, the opportunities for service in the American rabbinate are every bit as promising for women as they are for men. The flourishing of women rabbis that characterized the American rabbinate during the past two decades is very likely to continue as new avenues of rabbinic service beckon another generation of leaders.

Chapter II

My Religious Commitment

SHOULD AN ATHEIST OR AGNOSTIC CONSIDER THE RABBINATE?

Since one of the principal elements of Judaism is belief in the existence of God, an atheist—one for whom the word God has absolutely no meaning or relevance—should obviously refrain from choosing the rabbinate as a career. In the congregational rabbinate particularly, the rabbi officiates at religious services in which the reading of prayers is central, and it would be an act of the utmost hypocrisy for a *true* atheist to function in this context. The rabbi who is the representative of religious Judaism must have a deep and abiding desire to understand God. The rabbi's concept of God may grow with experience and study; God concepts may change radically or slightly. But the rabbi must have a profound belief in something greater than the human being that gives meaning and purpose to life and brings vitality and animation to all that exists. As the bedrock of this faith, the rabbi's idea of God gives shape to all of the other beliefs and acts of his or her rabbinate.

Judaism's God concepts have grown to maturity in its long history. Despite the diversity of approaches to gaining knowledge of God, whether rational, mystical, or existential, some basic beliefs have remained characteristic of it. Judaism teaches that God is One, and that Oneness is a Unity in which all else finds its being. In addition, there is an ethical side to

God to which the human being responds and which, in turn, responds to the human being. This religious philosophy is called ethical monotheism. Judaism envisages the human being and God as partners in the process of continuous creation; there is an interdependence of the human and the Divine in bringing about the rectification of the world. The Jew is aware of this dependence upon God and knows that the fulfillment of God's plan for humanity teaches that Israel received a unique revelation of God's nature. Orthodoxy holds that this revelation took place at one breakthrough in human consciousness at Mt. Sinai, with the giving of the Ten Commandments and the Torah. Conservatism, Reconstructionism, and Reform maintain that Israel's revelation is ongoing. Israel saw God in every moment of its history, not only at Sinai. This special awareness of God's mandates for humanity makes of Israel a "special people" (*am segulah*), whose task it is to live the truths of its vision and to teach them to others. Reform Judaism has called this the "mission of Israel" and points to this prophetic function as the chief reason for the necessary and continued existence of Judaism. A Jewish atheist, who would argue that the teachings of ethical monotheism and its corollary principles are "dead," is obviously misplaced in the rabbinate.

It is somewhat different with the young person who is an agnostic. It was Thomas H. Huxley who first spoke of "agnostics." He contrasted his knowledge of God with that of the Gnostics of the ancient world who claimed to have a special *gnosis* (knowledge) of God's nature. An *a-gnostic*, as Huxley taught, is someone who has no absolute, irrefutable knowledge of God. While *gnosis*, for the Orthodox group, might equal the revealed Torah at Sinai, which for them is absolute, that is not the case with Reform, Reconstructionist, or Conservative Judaism. Since God continues to exist, *gnosis* is not frozen, nor is truth concerning God bound securely in a book or series of books. The great medieval Jewish philosopher Maimonides (1135–1204 C.E.), when faced with the problem of defining God, would only say what God was not. He understood full well that defining God in absolute language limits our conception of the Divine. This was a form of agnosticism but within the general framework of the ongoing body of Jewish belief. I consider this type of Jewish agnosticism among the most serious of *religious* positions and intellectual commitments.

In many ways agnosticism corresponds to the major tendency of Jewish speculative thought since Maimonides. I have reference to the agnosticism that is convinced of the existence of some superior power, something that transcends earthly strivings and through which one discovers more about human existence, but concerning the full nature of which knowledge is incomplete. It has been a cardinal principle of Jewish philosophers, with few exceptions, not to close the discussion on theological issues, including the question of God's nature. Jewish philosophers realized that once they made a positive definition of God, subsequent new knowledge and experience would make it difficult to change a fixed concept.

Orthodox Judaism would take issue with the viewpoint just described and would maintain that only the accepted traditional God concept could qualify one as an Orthodox rabbinic candidate. In the Orthodox position, God is a supernatural being. It is only such a God that can command the human, and it is only to such a God that the human can respond through prayer. Reform Judaism, Reconstructionism, and the liberal wing of Conservative Judaism would be hospitable as well to the other expressions of one's ideas of God.

It is my conviction that a young man or woman seriously in search of God and unsure as yet of a full understanding of the Divine Voice may consider himself or herself a candidate for the rabbinate. One must, however, choose a seminary in which one's quest will not be misunderstood as basic doubt.

WHERE DO I STAND?

Am I Orthodox?

It is likely that if you are Orthodox, you know it! An Orthodox Jew scrupulously observes *halakhah*. This involves strict adherence to Jewish law and a host of customs that make up the life of the fully observant Jew. It is usual for the candidate for the Orthodox rabbinate to be a graduate of a Jewish parochial elementary school and high school known as a *yeshiva*. On occasion, candidates for the Orthodox rabbinate come from nonreligious homes or from the other branches of Judaism. In such instances, the candidate must somehow master the required traditional background materials. Other qualifications necessary to be considered Orthodox relate to theological beliefs and life attitudes.

The spectrum of affiliation in Orthodoxy is varied, and much depends upon whether one is ultra-Orthodox or modern Orthodox. The *Hasidic* groups would fall into the first category, whereas "Young Israel" might aptly fit the second. The ultra-Orthodox might well consider a member of Young Israel or a Yeshiva University graduate as a "reformer." Within the Orthodox community, then, are a right and a left wing as well as an ever-growing center that seeks to moderate divergent opinions. One finds this divergence of viewpoint reflected in numerous day schools that supply the Orthodox seminaries with rabbinic candidates. There are presently some 75,000 pupils in about 400 Orthodox day schools under various sponsorships in the United States and Canada.

Differences in viewpoint and custom exist among the Orthodox synagogues; for example, the *shtibl*-type synagogues, meeting in small rooms in which the vocal participation of the congregants defies any modicum of decorum, versus the modern Orthodox synagogue, where one hears the service conducted by a capable cantor with a trained voice, using mechanical acoustical equipment. The ultra-Orthodox synagogue separates men from women during worship, either by a partition through the middle of the synagogue or by a women's gallery. However, there are modern Orthodox synagogues where men and women are seated together, and where one finds decorum.

The term *Orthodox* is derived from the combination of two Greek words, *ortho*, meaning "right" or "proper," and *doxa*, meaning "opinion." The term was first employed by

Abraham Furtado, president of the Sanhedrin convoked by Napoleon, in Paris, in the year 1807. The term has more often been used as a descriptive one by those who are non-Orthodox, although today it is employed by many traditionalists to describe their system of practice and belief. Many Orthodox Jews prefer a different designation, such as "*Torah*-true Jews," or those who believe in *Torah im Derekh Eretz*, meaning "Torah together with secular knowledge." Rabbi Emanuel Rackman, a leading Orthodox thinker, made the following observation:

> Notwithstanding popular opinion to the contrary, Orthodox Judaism does not give its adherents unequivocal answers to the basic questions of life. Nor does it even prescribe for every situation in which the Jew may find himself. What it does have is religious, philosophical and ethical imperatives; these are often antithetical in character and man is rarely spared the onus of deliberate choice and decision. It is important to point this out for the benefit of those who are already committed to the Law as well as for those who are about to embrace it.

Rabbi Rackman has pointed out that "Judaism affords no escape from the awareness of reality or the exercise of reason. Indeed, the divinely revealed must be true—in the absolute sense—and what is absolutely true can be an anchor for emotional and intellectual security." That this position of the modern Orthodox movement is far from secure can be measured by the remarks of the late professor Leon Stitskin (1911–1978) of Yeshiva University. Addressing himself to the ultratraditionalist wing of his movement, he observed:

> There are those who would oppose a synthesis of Torah values with general knowledge (*Torah* and *Mada*) for fear of diluting the former. Yeshiva University has pursued a policy of blending the eternal verities of Torah with academic learning in order to develop a fully integrated personality.

Our Torah does not need to be sheltered or protected. Its abiding values are not only capable of withstanding the exigencies of surrounding cultures, but can help mold and humanize them. The impact of Torah verities are everlasting, meaningful and challenging.

To consider oneself Orthodox, allegiance must be given to certain cardinal principles as well as religious modes of conduct. Rabbi Leon Jung, a renowned Orthodox rabbi, maintained:

The one doctrine whence all arises is that of revelation ... what had been conveyed by Torah is not the fruit of Moses' genius nor the summing-up or restatement of the wisdom or insights of many, but the uncovering (that is what "reveal" means) of the nature of God and His role in the affairs of the cosmos and of men. The revelation of Sinai yielded the doctrine that God by His nature is unique and absolute. He is Law-giver and the Torah provides the vehicle whereby man can endeavor to imitate Him and His qualities of righteousness and mercy. It is necessary, therefore, to accept the Torah as a set of principles, a body of practice, as a faith and an attitude requiring "study as a method of worship" and "worship as a method of study." This is to lead to ethical consciousness and create the striving for a more perfect society. The Torah contains certain precepts grounded in the Five Books of Moses, supplemented by the teaching of the prophets, and the application of these teachings by the rabbis in an uninterrupted chain of activity spanning Judaism's history and "forming the skeleton of the national building." This complex of legal tradition shapes the *halakhah*, which is the Jewish way of life and which, based on its classic texts, is made applicable by certain prescribed procedures of interpretation to the new conditions in which the Jew finds himself.

It is a cardinal principle of Orthodoxy, wherein it differs perceptibly from Reform Judaism, that no Jew can lawfully put his or her own interpretation on *halakhah* according to individual insight and understanding of *halakhah*. This doctrine of revelation is the bedrock upon which Orthodoxy rests and from which its other facets of interpretation are derived. If you are an Orthodox Jew you believe that "*Torah*-true Judaism" is life and law that provides training and character and induces a total world view. Certain duties between God and the human being, between the human and his or her fellow ensue from this understanding of revelation. Among many laws and traditions, the Orthodox Jew is expected to adhere strictly to the dietary laws, the laws pertaining to the observance of the Sabbath and the holidays, the covering of the head at all times, daily worship, the wearing of phylacteries for the morning services with exceptions as the Law provides, and the wearing of *tzitzit*, a garment with fringes to bring one to the constant awareness of the presence of God in one's life.

The written law and the oral law represent the compendium of Jewish law and life and are to be understood in their fundamental essence. Higher criticism of the Bible, which would tend to show that the Five Books of Moses represent a collection of documents spanning a thousand years of creativity, would be precluded as a vehicle of understanding Jewish tradition. Orthodoxy, then, is as much a psychology as a philosophy of life. Persons who are committed to the many precepts of Jewish law, and are willing to live by them, may consider themselves and be considered by others as Orthodox Jews.

Am I a Reform Jew?
Reform Judaism is the vigorous and dynamic faith that first attempted to reconcile Judaism with the modern world. Reform claims more than one million adherents on the American continent alone and is the oldest organized religious movement in America. Although the roots of

Reform Judaism go back to the beginning of the nineteenth century in Germany, the movement grew to maturity and its greatest growth in America. The brilliant organizing genius of Isaac Mayer Wise established the Union of American Hebrew Congregations in Cincinnati, in 1873. Its purpose, as stated in its constitution, is "to encourage and aid the organization and development of Jewish congregations; to promote Jewish education and enrich and intensify Jewish life; to maintain the Hebrew Union College–Jewish Institute of Religion; and to foster other activities for the perpetuation and advancement of Judaism." In 1875 Wise founded the Hebrew Union College, whose purpose was to train rabbis nurtured on American soil. Wise was the first to see that if Judaism in America were to have a future, it needed to be sustained by American Jews and could no longer rely upon European religious leadership. Little did Wise, or any of his contemporaries, realize how fateful such a prediction would be. With the decimation of the great centers of European Jewry during the Nazi era, America emerged as the greatest center of Jewish life and learning in the world.

Wise, from the outset, was interested in creating a *"Minhag*-America"; that is, an American way of living a Jewish life. His original efforts were directed at unifying the rabbinate and congregations in America. His vision was grand, but the realities of the situation militated against its fulfillment. Wise founded the Central Conference of American Rabbis in 1889. Contrary to popular opinion, Reform Judaism has never been of only one religious viewpoint. While it has adopted several platforms of belief—one in 1885 known as the Pittsburgh Platform, another in 1937 known as the Columbus Platform, and a third in 1976 called not a platform but a Centenary Perspective—Reform Judaism has remained alive to the theological and social currents of America and the world. If there has been a single characteristic of Reform Judaism, it has been its impatience with the status quo. Recently Rabbi Alexander M. Schindler, president of the Union of American Hebrew Congregations, expressed this view most eloquently:

Reform Judaism is undisputedly authentic, profoundly true to the spirit of the Jewish tradition. Let no one denigrate its worth. It has contributed immeasurably to the creative continuity of the Jewish people.

Whereas the Orthodox movement emphasizes "*Torah*-true Judaism," and Conservative Judaism, in the words of Solomon Schechter, extols "Law-mindedness" in the rabbi, the Reform movement underscores the rabbi and the prophetic tradition. The Reform movement is always attempting to develop new forms of expression for Judaism's ancient faith, creed, and ritual. It was in the nature of the early reformers to be drastic in their attempt to strip Judaism of seemingly irrelevant externalities which, like the husk of a cob of corn, concealed its kernel. It was the viewpoint of the Reform movement that Judaism could not survive in the modern world in its ancient ghetto garb. On the other hand, Reform attempted critically to understand the history and evolution of Jewish religious thought and practice. Its rabbis were pioneers in what has been called "the scholarly study of Judaism" (*Wissenschaft des Judentums*). Through scholarly inquiry into Israel's ancient past, it was discovered that Judaism in its biblical and talmudic period was a vital religion, creating new concepts and practices from within as time and circumstance required.

Reform Judaism's concept of revelation reflected the belief that revelation was not frozen in one moment of history on Sinai, but was an ongoing process in which each generation participated and found its own truths. Because Reform Judaism was born in the Age of Enlightenment, which relied heavily on the spirit of reason, it was believed that revelation was progressive and that each generation could stand on the shoulders of its predecessors to see newer and greater truths for Israel and all of humankind. It was therefore incumbent upon Reform Judaism to attempt to reconcile Jewish belief with modern thought and to welcome all truth, whether ancient or modern. Wise taught: "Judaism ... maintains that God is no less revealed in nature and history than in the

Bible, and His operations must be observed and His perfection studied in all departments of revelation.''
The temper of Reform Judaism insisted upon a rational faith for the modern Jew. In its eagerness to make Judaism once again credible, it removed much from the area of ceremony that seemed a hindrance to this quest. Rabbi Solomon Freehof has observed that early Reform Judaism

... considered the ceremonial system to be trivializing of the noble teaching of Judaism. Even the deep learning involved in the study of it was looked upon as a wastage of intellectual capacity, an alienation of the broader culture of the modern world. This antiritual attitude seemed to be confirmed by events in Orthodoxy itself, for in wider and wider Orthodox circles the very spiritual basis of the old ritual rapidly seeped away. Fewer and fewer children of Israel continued to believe that these observances had come to us as a genuine mandate from God. As long as Jews did believe that, as they did for centuries, then all of each day's ritual was truly a pageant dedicated to the Omnipresent, but once they ceased to believe that, it did become mere routine and blind piety.

It was for this reason that the Reform movement sought compatibility with new thought rather than with tradition. The pioneer German reformer Rabbi Abraham Geiger's motto was: "To search in the past, to live in the present, to build for the future." It is that credo which Reform Judaism has attempted to hold firmly before its inner eye.

The advocates of Reform in Germany revised the traditional prayerbook, putting much of the liturgy in the vernacular and excluding from it ritual and ideas they believed to be outmoded. The ceremony of Bar Mitzvah, which had become routinized, was supplemented by the Confirmation. It was first introduced for boys and then expanded to include girls. Despite great opposition to it, the ceremony rapidly became popular and was adopted by many congregations whose ritual was otherwise according to tradition. The inclusion of girls in Confirmation came to symbolize the equality of women in religion and their importance in the perpetuation of Jewish life. The reformers eliminated the women's gallery as well as the whole mentality that made women second-class religious citizens. Reform Judaism returned to the biblical calendar in its scheduling of the festivals and of the New Year. It rejected the mind-set that made belief in miracles mandatory. It removed the obligatory character of the dietary laws, as well as the notion of the resurrection of the body after death. Reform emphasized the need to observe the Sabbath and the Holy Days but made room for contemporary interpretation of the festivals and life-cycle ceremonies of the Jew.

Because Reform Judaism was born in a century of unbridled hope in the capacity of every man and woman to better his or her condition, the notion of "a messianic era" instead of faith in a personal messiah was advocated, particularly by Abraham Geiger. This was viewed as an age in which there was to be universal righteousness, fellowship, and peace. It was, in fact, an idea that had originally been voiced by the prophets of ancient Israel and had also been taught by the rabbis of the talmudic era. Reform Judaism made much of the prophetic teaching that Israel was God's elected people and had a universal mission in the world. It was for this reason that a return to Palestine was negated in early Reform theology and an anti-Zionist element was included in its formulations.

A change in viewpoint on Zionism was brought about and incorporated into the Columbus Platform of 1937. It reads:

> In all lands where our people live, they assume and seek to share loyally the full duties and responsibilities of citizenship and to create seats of knowledge and religion. In the rehabilitation of Palestine, a land hallowed by memories and hopes, we behold the promise of renewed life for many of our brethren. We affirm the obligation of all Jewry to aid in its upbuilding as a Jewish homeland by endeavoring to make it not only to be a haven or refuge for

the oppressed but also a center of Jewish culture and spiritual life.

The sentiment of the Central Conference of American Rabbis is today preponderantly in favor of some type of Zionist philosophy. Today, many Reform rabbis are members of the Association of Reform Zionists of America (ARZA).

Reform Judaism's commitment to the prophetic ideal of social justice led it from the very outset to pioneer in social action. The Columbus Platform's plea that "Judaism seeks the attainment of a just society by the application of its teachings through the economic order, industry and commerce, and through national and international affairs" propelled the members of the Conference into the eye of the hurricane of social change. While it is common today to see rabbis of all branches of Judaism involved in social action, this was not always the case. Reform rabbis were pace-setters among the Jewish clergy in attempting to extend the doctrines of prophetic teaching into the lifeblood of society. Rabbi Stephen S. Wise, founder of the Jewish Institute of Religion, a dynamic and magnetic leader and organizer, was perhaps foremost as an exemplar of the prophetic tradition. The Religious Action Center of the Union of American Hebrew Congregations, in Washington, D.C., is the first, and presently the only, such establishment in American Jewish religious life, dramatizing to the nation that Jews are concerned with the moral issues of legislation, in the rightness of the law as well as its efficacy.

The candidate who aspires to the Reform rabbinate must have a hunger for a deep knowledge of the ideas of Judaism. It is also vitally important to know the world in which we live, intimately and in a far-reaching way. He must have an "informed kind of *emunah*," enlightened faith. Dr. Nelson Glueck (1900–1971), my predecessor as president of the Hebrew Union College–Jewish Institute of Religion, a great scholar and archaeologist, observed:

> Reform Judaism is often misunderstood and misrepresented as being minimal in its demands. In its truest

definition, it has ever insisted not upon less dedication, less information, less observance, but upon richer understanding of, and warmer devotion to, the fundamentals of our faith. Reform Judaism remains and has always been concerned with the totality of all of Israel, in whose destiny it is intertwined and in whose hope it sees its brightest future.

Do I Belong with the Conservatives?

The hub of the Conservative movement in the Western Hemisphere is the Jewish Theological Seminary of America, situated in New York and presided over by Dr. Ismar Schorsch. The Seminary came into being as a reaction against the liberality of the Reform movement, as expressed in the Pittsburgh Platform of 1885. In that Platform, Reform Judaism asserted itself primarily as a religious group, denying the implications of nationhood and the aspiration to restore the Jewish national home in Palestine. It also severed, in principle, the binding power of Jewish traditional law and dropped many observances that had come to permeate Jewish life. Disturbed by these breaks with traditional Judaism, a small group of English-speaking rabbis decided to form a theological seminary that would oppose these tendencies and would act as a counterbalance to the Hebrew Union College. The Jewish Theological Seminary opened in 1887, and in 1902 the distinguished Rabbi Solomon Schechter, who was a Reader in Rabbinics at Cambridge University, was invited to become its president. This exemplary scholar and administrator guided the institution to a place of great prominence as the primary exponent of what is called Conservative Judaism.

From the outset, and for a long time thereafter, the religious leaders of the Seminary made no attempt to create a new movement or to follow the precedent set by the Central Conference of American Rabbis in framing a platform of common beliefs. The Seminary's slogan was "catholic Israel," and it appealed to a segment of Jews for whom Reform Judaism was too radical and Orthodoxy too traditional. The majority of its supporters came from Eastern

Europe, especially Jews of Poland, Russia, Hungary, and Rumania. The Conservatives refused to articulate a systematic program and were often attacked by the Orthodox as being a timid Reform. The formulators of the Conservative position, particularly Dr. Schechter, followed a pragmatic approach in their attempt to weave an American Judaism for traditionalists who wanted to live a Jewish life within their American environment. The architects of Conservatism drew together a consensus of viewpoints that still operates today.

Reaching back to the platform of the Theological Seminary in Breslau, the ideas of its intellectual leader, Zacharias Frankel, Conservative Judaism expounded the position of "positive-historical Judaism." Frankel hoped to suggest by this unusual designation the process of change within traditional Judaism. He championed the view that Judaism is the product of historical development. Frankel held it to be wrong to surrender the primacy of the Hebrew language in worship for the sake of comprehension of the liturgy. He defended many other traditional beliefs but insisted also on the need for scientific research. Since Judaism is the product of an evolutionary process, an attempt must be made to understand its growth and development. Frankel also underscored the importance of the national elements in Judaism that Rabbi Solomon Schechter later used in his own formulation of the idea of "religious nationalism."

Ahad Ha-Am, who was born in Russia and died in Palestine, developed the viewpoint that Judaism has a culture as well as a religion. He was the architect of the philosophy that came to be known as "Cultural Zionism," in which Eretz Yisrael was viewed as the spiritual center of the Jewish people. Renewed cultural activity and the recreation of Hebrew language and literature could most naturally take place there. He also emphasized the ethical character of Judaism. Utilizing this approach, a disciple of his, Professor Israel Friedlander (1876–1920), a faculty member of the Jewish Theological Seminary, developed the position that Judaism is a complete culture and not merely a creed. Professor Louis Ginzberg (1873–1953), a great talmudic scholar, continued in the tradition of Frankel to develop critical methods of studying rabbinic literature and law. He stressed the need to interpret the ideas and practices of Jewish tradition.

The Seminary demands some basic requirements of its applicants for the rabbinate: observance of the dietary laws, the Sabbath, and festivals, daily prayers, and conduct according to Jewish law and tradition. Rabbi Robert Gordis capsulized the basic philosophy of Conservative Judaism as follows: "Judaism is the evolving religious culture and civilization of the Jewish people." The practical implications of this point of view have made Conservative Judaism adaptive to its American environment and have been able to make its program flexible. It is becoming increasingly difficult to differentiate between a traditional-minded Reform Jew and a liberally oriented Conservative Jew. Conservatives have accepted mixed seating at worship services and many other practices that had previously been labeled "Reform." The services are conducted in English and in Hebrew, and the average sermon topic of the Conservative rabbi is closely akin to that of his Reform counterpart. Basically, what still differentiate the Conservative and the Reform Jew, aside from the institutional commitments that exist, are a temper of mind regarding the uses of tradition and law and the obligatory nature of some observance.

Among the Conservative rabbis I have known, I have found internal differences on many theological issues. The ideology of some Conservative rabbis is more radical than that of some Reform rabbis, and some Reform rabbis espouse a theology much more traditional than that of some Conservative rabbis. In time, a reappraisal of the respective positions of the Conservative and Reform movements will undoubtedly have to be made, and perhaps a real rapprochement of many Conservative and Reform rabbis can be effected.

The key issue separating Conservative and Reform rabbis is the binding authority of *halakhah*. The Conservative movement has loosened the thread of *halakhah* considerably so as to become vulnerable in the eyes of the Orthodox. On the other hand, Reform rabbis, having broken altogether with the binding nature of *halakhah*, often find the position of Conservative rabbis to be inconsistent. Rabbi Gordis has summarized the position of the Conservatives very well in his statement:

> If we surrender our adherence to Jewish Law, we shall be courting anarchy; if we suffer it to petrify, we shall be inviting disaster. Our goal is loyalty to an evolving Law, which is the will of God as revealed through the experience of Israel. If this statement represents your view on Jewish law and experience, and you adhere to otherwise traditional norms and practices, then you are indeed of the Conservative persuasion and should consider yourself a Conservative Jew.

Do I Belong with the Reconstructionist Movement?

Professor Mordecai M. Kaplan (1881–1983), a scholar and thinker, founded the Reconstructionist movement. Reconstructionism was meant to be a pervasive philosophy of Jewish life whose teachings could be inserted into the other movements. Reconstructionism is a Jewish humanist philosophy in which Judaism is viewed as a religious civilization. A civilization implies a cultural and linguistic content and is concerned with the totality of existence. Reconstructionism has accented long-neglected facets of Jewish culture, such as music and art, which at one time were part and parcel of a full Jewish life. The Reconstructionist philosophy stresses the importance of cultural forms in shaping the identity of the modern Jew, such as the rebirth of Hebrew as a spoken tongue and as a source for new creativity. Judaism, which is seen as an evolving religious civilization of the Jewish people, features the people as the central factor of Jewish experience. Dr. Kaplan focused upon the nature of Jewish peoplehood, which is also the bearer of the Jewish civilizational mode.

On the question of the nature of God, Dr. Kaplan believed that ancient nomenclature is no longer valid. For him, God is a process in which the cosmic principle of polarity operates. Subjectively, God is experienced as that power within us which makes us redeem our society and our human condition. This power leads us to concretize Jewish ethical norms into daily experience. In his view of God, Kaplan is far removed from the official positions of both the Conservative and Reform movements, and yet, paradoxically, he enjoys an influential following of both Conservative and Reform rabbis who have embraced this theology.

In 1968 the Reconstructionist movement founded a rabbinical college in Philadelphia.

MY VALUES AND THE RABBINIC CALLING

Often, the religious rearing of childhood undergoes painstaking reappraisal as one grows to maturity, and the beliefs of one's youth suffer drastic revision. In conjunction with this appraisal of theological position must come the honest evaluation of one's values and whether they are in harmony with the rabbinic calling. More than in most callings, the rabbi, in life and thought, represents the teaching of Judaism. The rabbis of the Mishnah observed, ''Not learning but doing is the chief thing.'' What the rabbi stands for can be just as important as what the rabbi knows. The talmudic sage Rabbah instructs us that ''any rabbi whose inside is not like his outside is no rabbi.'' The revered Rabbi Leo Baeck taught: ''The message is not the sermon of a preacher but the man himself. The man must be the message. The rabbi must not deliver a message, he must deliver himself.''

One of the essential characteristics of a candidate considering rabbinic study is idealism. By that I do not mean to imply that one is required to be deaf to worldly demands or to one's practical needs and those of one's family. Asceticism is not an ideal of Judaism. Judaism expounds an indissoluble unity of body and soul, heart and mind. A rabbi's idealism must be a genuine part of his or her personality and not some accrued, belated affectation. Rabbis must express themselves not only in synagogue or at stated times, but through the totality of everyday life.

Because the rabbi must be an idealist, certain practical

consequences flow from this position. The ancient rabbis implied by their teaching that the scholar of Torah, to achieve the maximum independence in the quest for truth, must reduce material requirements to the absolute minimum. One may find it necessary to sacrifice worldly goods for the preservation of integrity. The rabbinic student who envisages the rabbinate as a vocation from which to amass sizeable amounts of money is sorely misguided. Very few rabbis remain in the rabbinate because of its material rewards. Because of the caliber of the average rabbi, he could do at least as well financially in some other vocation; the monetary reward is hardly an inducement to remain in a difficult and immensely challenging calling. The rabbi's primary incentive is idealism.

Rabbi Abraham J. Feldman (1893–1977) once highlighted two ideals which, in his opinion, constitute the indispensable minimum in the rabbinate, "To serve God and to serve God's people Israel constitute the principal tasks of the rabbinate. All other fascinations there are about this profession do not in themselves constitute a valid reason for entering it." Rabbi Feldman asked the question, why "serve Israel"? He answered that we start where the roots of Judaism are. We begin a structure by laying the foundations and gradually building upward. It is when we destroy a structure that demolition is started from the top and proceeds toward the foundations, as when a tree begins to die it withers first at the top. In the constructive work of the rabbinate, the foundation is service to the people of Israel. Although the rabbi is ordained by a particular movement, to be of specific service to it, his or her own concept of the rabbinate must embrace service to the totality of Israel.

An ideal of the rabbi, without which service to the Jewish people is impossible, is a love and respect for fellow human beings. Far from lording it over a congregation or institution, a rabbi must be capable of entering into genuine dialogue with congregants and associates alike. It must be remembered that, apart from the solitary hours the rabbi spends in pursuit of knowledge, rabbinic work is with people, for "life is with people.'' The rabbi conducts services, officiates at weddings and funerals, names and blesses newborn children, visits the sick and the bereaved, counsels the troubled, confers with those who seek advice for important decisions in their lives, addresses gatherings, and participates in dedications and a host of other congregational and communal functions. A person who dislikes people will be a miserable rabbi; one would be tormented by the many hours that must be spent as a public figure and the endless effort that must be expended with others in the day-to-day flow of rabbinic work.

The love of study must be part of the rabbi's system of values and represent the bedrock upon which preaching and lectures are based. One who teaches but does not study will soon be like an empty vessel, resounding with hollow echoes. Often in the solitude of study, among books of great wisdom, new insights are born and new dedication wells up, enabling the rabbi to be more effective and creative. Although the intellectual demands made upon the rabbi may vary from congregation to congregation, it is becoming increasingly evident that the preponderance of Jewish congregants are college graduates and represent a wide spectrum of professional attainment. Hardly a congregation exists that does not have within it college professors, lawyers, doctors, aerospace technicians, physicists, and members of many other emerging professions. The level of their education is graduate and postgraduate, and the rabbi must attempt to reach them through intellectually acceptable addresses and sermons. The rabbi is fortunate who learns from congregants even while teaching them.

The rabbi must be a forceful person, capable of articulating thoughts with precision and conviction. A terrible temptation in the rabbinate is to hanker after meaningless popularity and admiration. For this reason, I feel that a candidate for the rabbinate must be essentially a modest person who will not seek admirers but attempt to gain followers. While every rabbi is, of course, human and imperfect, his or her sense of values must be such as to counterbalance the vulgarities in contemporary life. The rabbi's eye must be fixed on the timeless and not only on the timely, and that requires great courage. Rabbi Robert Hammer, in an article, "Character-destroying Factors in the Rabbinate," wrote:

> The rabbinate is one of the world's most dangerous ways of life for it makes demands and imposes stresses that are both impossible and contradictory . . . The authority that one must assume endangers humility, the righteousness with which one must act is often too close to self-righteousness. The rabbinic character is distorted by these conflicting attitudes toward the rabbi. A rabbi is too freely criticized, but also too freely flattered; too fiercely possessed and too coldly deplored.

The rabbi must be very clear as to what he or she believes to be matters of principle, and these convictions must never be compromised. Neither adulation nor criticism should swerve a rabbi from what he or she knows to be right; a rabbi must be willing to live and dramatize through teaching and personal conduct.

Another constellation of values revolves around the rabbi's basic world outlook. Primary concern is directed toward leading a religious life imbued with Jewish faith and values. This requires a sense of inner piety, which should deepen through the years. The rabbi has to be willing and able to officiate at services and at the life-cycle ceremonies of congregants. These cannot be merely perfunctory rites and rituals. Each occasion presents a new challenge, and it is supremely important for the rabbi to find the inner capacity to make these events meaningful. The uninspired rabbi, the cold officiator, the marriage and burial clerk mentality reflects a rabbi who is devoid of personal piety or who has lost the capacity to find religious meaning in the events that confront our daily life.

Having delineated these general values necessary to the

rabbinic calling, we might now establish an additional checklist of helpful attributes.

1. A rabbi must speak and write well. Words are tools for imparting knowledge; consequently, a rabbi must strive to master the techniques necessary for conveying his or her thoughts. I shall never forget the first sermon I submitted to my teacher of homiletics, Dr. Israel Bettan (1889–1957) of blessed memory. Scrawled on the back of the sermon was the note, "See me!" With great trepidation, I went to see Dr. Bettan to hear his criticism. In his inimitable style, he commented on this or that passage and then finally he threw the caveat. "Your style, my friend, is so heavy and cumbersome. Why don't you write like this: 'The Lord is my shepherd, I shall not want'—crystal-clear!" I have never been able to forget Dr. Bettan's advice, either in the preparation of a sermon or of a manuscript. Whatever is imparted must be crystal-clear, and that involves considerable effort.

2. The rabbinic candidate must possess the capacity for empathy. Rabbi Robert Katz, Professor of Human Relations at the Hebrew Union College, says that "when we experience empathy we feel as if we are experiencing someone else's feelings as our own. We see, we feel, we respond, and we understand as if we were, in fact, the other person. We stand in his shoes. We get under his skin." For the rabbi to counsel and help others, it is necessary to understand the situation of the other person. Our sages put it this way: "Do not judge another person until you stand in his place." The capacity to feel empathy is vital to the rabbinate.

3. Patience with the failings of others and humility about one's own accomplishments or feelings of superiority are very necessary. The rabbi who is a teacher knows that as a flower comes to blossom but slowly, so does understanding in the mind and heart of the pupil. It may take years to convince some members of the

congregation of the correctness of a cherished viewpoint. In the process, the rabbi must always work with awareness of his or her own fallibility, mindful that, indeed, the views of others may be more correct than one's own.

4. A good heart is indispensable to the rabbinate. The great sage Rabbi Johanan ben Zakkai once exhorted his disciples to go into the world and see what it was that a human being should cherish the most. The disciples returned and gave their report. One said, "A generous eye." Another said, "A loyal friend." A third said, "A good neighbor." A fourth said, "The gift of foresight." The last, Rabbi Elazer, said, "A good heart." It is reported that Rabbi Johanan said, "I prefer the answer of Rabbi Elazar ben Arach to those of the rest of you, for in his words yours are included." In modern terms, having a good heart means being a good human being. The rabbi's own generosity and acts of goodness must rise spontaneously from within. The rabbi who is a "mensch" normally judges people favorably and gives them the benefit of the doubt. Rabbi Feldman observed, "The rabbi must be generous even to a fault in judging and evaluating people, especially in *voiced* judgments." No sensible rabbi would speak ill of anyone in a eulogy; the same is true for the living.

5. Be a lover of peace! Peace does not mean appeasement, nor does it mean unprincipled compromise. The sage Hillel enjoined his colleagues to be "of the disciples of Aaron, loving peace and pursuing it." Peace must be a paramount value in a rabbi's life, and since it does not come easily, it must be pursued.

6. In a rabbi, a great capacity for friendship is vital. This does not imply descending to the lowest denominator of hilarity, or rolling up one's sleeves to become one of the gang. It does imply the capacity to trust and be trusted. Carl Hermann Voss' fascinating book, *Rabbi and Minister*, depicts the friendship of Rabbi Stephen S.

Wise and the great Protestant minister John Haynes Holmes. Their cooperative ventures in religious activity in New York transformed the moral face of that city. Wise, particularly, had a tremendous capacity for friendship. Stories were legion as to his phenomenal memory for the names and faces of even casual acquaintances. Because of his deep interest in people, Wise got to know them or at least something very important about them. Thereafter, whenever he met them, he could recall what it was that had tied him to these people. This was not a sham interest but a real concern for the people who entered the orbit of his life. Aristotle thought the capacity for friendship to be the single most important quality in human existence. In the rabbinate, it is a prized gift.

7. No rabbi has the right to be a snob. Within the rabbi's republic he must be a democrat. The rabbi may not succumb to what the late Rabbi Maurice Eisendrath (1902–1973) called "the grievous failings of American culture—the worship of money, power, status, success—..." The rabbi must be conditioned to show no overt favoritism to those who are well-heeled nor to ignore those who are down-at-heel. The rabbi's time and energy are available to all congregants equally. As a religious leader, the rabbi ought not to favor powerful families in the congregation or important members of the community. A colleague of mine relates the story of a very important member of his congregation whose daughter had decided to be married on a certain date. The rabbi's calendar was already full for that day, and he could not officiate at the ceremony without breaking a previous commitment. Some pressure was brought upon him to cancel his original date, but he categorically refused. Contrary to what might have been expected, when he explained the ethics of the situation to the outraged "important member," he won the respect and admiration of that man, as well as of the board of his congregation. The rabbi is more than a

"profile in courage"; a rabbi must indeed be the
embodiment of courage.

8. A sense of humor is indispensable in the rabbinate. It is
necessary to deflate a profession that is highly charged
with emotion and propels the rabbi from one tension-
laden situation to another. The rabbi may not take
himself or herself too seriously for fear of becoming a
figure of pomposity and, ultimately, an object of
derision. After all, the rabbi is human and capable of
making mistakes—sometimes many of them, but it is
hoped not the same ones too often. Frequently, a
rabbi's sense of humor can take the wind out of the sails
of animosity and create an atmosphere of relaxed
amiability. I remember vividly one night when Dr.
Stephen S. Wise was addressing a large audience in New
York. He was speaking against Nazism. Earlier that
evening he had received a threat to his life if he were to
go through with his address. Dr. Wise arose and, in his
inimitable grand style, announced to the public: "I
understand that an attempt will be made on my life
tonight. If the assassin is in the audience, I beg him to
shoot now; I should hate to be interrupted in the middle
of my oration." The instantaneous response to Dr.
Wise's sense of humor calmed the situation and, since
the joke he told was on himself, he could well afford to
enjoy his own laughter.

SUCCESS IN THE RABBINATE

The rabbinate is a profession composed of mortals.
Although most rabbis seek to emulate scholars and saints,
they are very *human* beings. With the exception of the ultra-
Orthodox rabbi who wears a distinctive garb reminiscent of
medieval Europe, most rabbis don't "look like rabbis."
Although the good Lord has given to a handful of my
colleagues the features of Michelangelo's Moses, most rabbis
look and dress like ordinary human beings. Without the

telltale pulpit robe, the rabbi is indistinguishable in a crowd. What differentiates the rabbi from others is his or her work.

Very few rabbis would admit to "receiving a call" from God or some divine power in the way that term is used in the Christian ministry. By contrast, Jews speak of "studying for the rabbinate." The aspiration to be a teacher of Judaism often serves as the motivating thrust to engage in rabbinic study.

The late Rabbi Edgar F. Magnin (1890–1984), with whom I often discussed the question of what it takes to be a successful rabbi, argued that the rabbinate is essentially an art. He made the distinction between being arty and an artist; between affectation and basic drama; between a false stentorian voice and speaking with conviction. If the rabbinate is indeed an art, then we can measure it only by the artists who practice it. The consummate artistry of a Joshua Loth Liebman, a Milton Steinberg, a Rav Kook, and countless others is deserving of emulation. There is a considerable difference between emulation and imitation. A great rabbi used to admonish his younger imitators, "One of me is quite enough, perhaps too many. Be yourself!" He would also advise, "A voice of honey is no substitute for the salt of thought." The temptation to follow the patterns of "successful" rabbis is always present and represents a great pitfall for young colleagues. Whatever you have to give to the rabbinate is derived from your individuality, from the way you put together the great themes of Jewish history and play them through your unique person.

How shall we measure success in the rabbinate? It is clear from our tradition, as our sages have said, "Take heed of the children of the poor, for from them will come forth the word of God." The rabbinate rewarded those who were part of the aristocracy of learning and who possessed the qualities of self-reliance and self-respect. Indicative of these qualities is a story recorded in our tradition of a certain rabbi who, having accepted an invitation to dine with the political leader of his day (Patriarch), responded, "I do not want to deprive His Excellency of the honor of my presence." This was not meant

to be an arrogant statement, but one that attempted to inform
the Patriarch that it was an equal and not an underling whom
he had invited. Arrogance among the aristocrats of learning
was condemned. The sage Hillel said that whoever brags
about his reputation will in the end lose it. Louis Ginzberg, in
his classic volume *Students, Scholars and Saints*, discussed
the authority of the *Talmid hakham*, and deduced that the
rabbinic scholar drew his power

... neither from the existence of a learned class nor in the
constitution of the Jewish community. It was rather the
personality of the scholar that gave him his prominent
position. He was one whose mission was proclaimed by
nothing in his apparel, but whose life and words made
themselves felt in all hearts and consciences. He was of the
people, and the people recognized themselves in him.

The times in which we live present some distorted images of
success. Too often the second question that a rabbi is asked,
after being introduced, is "How large is your congregation?"
If the number is large, the assumption is that the rabbi is the
recipient of a large salary, and the rabbi's position is summed
up in the mind of the questioner as a "success." Although
some rabbis do measure their own success by the standards
of a materialistic society, the vast majority weigh their
achievements on other scales. In 1945 Joseph Zeitlin
published the first major sociological study of the values of
the American rabbinate. *Disciples of the Wise: The Religious
and Social Opinions of American Rabbis* (New York: 1945)
came to the following findings and conclusions:

The preponderant majority of the American rabbinate is
committed to a utilitarian moral philosophy.
    The rabbinate is well-nigh unanimous in its conviction that
religion, to be a vital force, must identify itself with recon-
structive social movements ...
    A large proportion of the rabbinate see socially reconstruc-
tive implications in the spirit of Judaism ...

The rabbinate in all its wings is preponderantly in favor of increasing social responsibility for the welfare and security of the individual . . .

The rabbinate in all its wings is virtually unanimous in favoring the extension of the scope of social responsibility, for education beyond the prevailing level . . .

Issues falling within the areas of philosophy of Jewish life, theology, and the social function of religion receive considerable preaching emphasis . . .

Moral principles constitute the ultimate basis of validity of any political, economic, and social arrangements . . .

Democracy is the only pattern of social relations that constitutes a des. gn for human living . . .

Imperialism abroad and oppression and inequalities at home that are based on racial differences are contradictory to the concepts of religion.

The Jewish world has changed radically since Zeitlin's study appeared. I hope that some ambitious sociologist will soon examine the American rabbinate's religious and social opinions as they exist today, over forty years later. The comparison would be fascinating. Nevertheless, the American rabbi in the late 1980's still measures his/her success or failure by the extent to which the ideology of Judaism has been translated into the lifestream of society. The greater the rabbi's artistry in imparting Judaism in all its ramifications, the greater the rabbi. One must measure by the only standard that truly matters: the mandates of the "disciples of the wise."

Chapter III

Studying for the Rabbinate

PERSONAL QUALIFICATIONS

Preparing for the modern rabbinate usually means graduation from one of the seminaries representing the major branches of Judaism. The person who plans to make a career in the rabbinate should begin serious exploration of that choice with one of the alumni of the seminary at which application will be made. Normally, this would be the student's congregational rabbi, or the director of the Hillel Foundation, or some other active rabbi in Jewish communal work. A potential student will receive sound advice from a seasoned counselor, who will normally also put the prospective candidate in touch with the Director of Admissions of the seminary being considered.

In addition to the desire to be a rabbi, the prospective rabbinic student must check his or her own personal qualifications to see whether, by interest or aptitude, it will be possible to complete the seminary's training program. The potential student should be sure of possessing a consuming and abiding interest in Jewish affairs. Does he or she feel a strong bond of affection for fellow Jews everywhere? Is he or she anxious to lead and to help them? Is he or she convinced that Judaism, and his or her own specific religious way of life, can help modern Jews live more meaningfully? Does he or she want to interpret and teach Judaism in a manner that will make it come alive for the modern Jew?

A future rabbi must believe that there is a Power within human life and a universe within which all men and women can cooperate to strengthen themselves by building a better world. Does the candidate have an insatiable curiosity about things Jewish and about the world in which we live? Does he or she possess the necessary human qualities such as empathy, compassion, patience, tolerance of criticism, and general psychological stability? Does the potential student recognize that the rabbinate is not an easy profession and that it is hardly likely that one will grow rich in it? While the rabbi may surely expect a decent standard of living and economic security, is the candidate prepared to place this in relation to the other values that should properly make the rabbinate an attractive field of endeavor?

Toward the fulfillment of ideals, is the candidate for rabbinic school prepared to work long and hard hours? Does he or she realize that rabbinic life is a public life and that, very much like the physician, the rabbi is virtually on call? Is he or she aware that his or her family will also often be on public display? If the prospective candidate can answer most of these questions in the affirmative, then he or she is ready to consider the requirements of the chosen seminary and to receive its advice and counsel.

In addition to certain motivational factors relating to the candidate's personal qualifications are the considerations of physical and psychological fitness. Most of the seminaries require a physical examination of entering students, which informs the school administration whether a candidate has a clean bill of health or has some restriction on physical activity. The Admissions Committee of the seminary must then determine whether or not the candidate is capable of carrying out the long and taxing course of study without incurring undue physical strain and impairment of health.

Students who pass the physical examination also undergo, in most seminaries, a psychological test. The purpose of this test is not merely to screen out emotionally unfit people, but also to give an indication of the personal problems and limitations a candidate may have. Students of the prerequisite intellectual ability and emotional stability usually clear this part of the admissions procedure without difficulty. The respective seminaries place varying degrees of emphasis on such tests. The HUC-JIR and the JTS have increasingly placed a high degree of value upon them, considering them indicators of fitness for a rabbinic career. With notable exceptions, the student has arrived at a theological preference in his or her own mind before making application to one of the seminaries. A student's application is normally sponsored by an alumnus of the school, and this presupposes an acquaintance with the candidate for admission. Usually a recommendation for admission is not enough. Application forms are required to be submitted, giving some detailed personal information on one's background and education. Preparation for admission to the rabbinic schools varies considerably from seminary to seminary. The greater the candidate's background in Hebrew and in general Judaica, the more advanced is his or her standing upon admission. All of the major seminaries, however, have made provision for the student who comes to them with no linguistic background, or with no more than a cursory acquaintance with the traditions of Judaism. For such candidates, special orientation programs are conducted, and normally the course of study is longer than that of the student who comes with adequate preparation.

EDUCATIONAL BACKGROUND AND APTITUDE

Two questions are usually asked by an undergraduate student who plans to be a candidate for rabbinic study: What shall be my major in college, and how as an undergraduate may I better prepare myself for the seminary of my choice? As a condition for admission to the rabbinic department, which is a graduate school, the major seminaries require completion of the baccalaureate degree.

The JTS and the HUC-JIR place a particularly high premium on a well-rounded liberal arts education. This requirement is predicated on the assumption that the modern rabbi must be able to relate Jewish knowledge to general culture. Therefore, they require preparation in the fields of philosophy, history, psychology, language and literature, and the sciences. Since the rabbi must communicate well, careful attention should be paid to formal courses in English composition and literature. Both seminaries reserve the right, upon examination of a candidate's credentials, to require additional liberal arts courses should there be deficiencies in this area.

After all the required transcripts, recommendations, and other documents are in the hands of the Director of Admissions, the usual admission procedure provides for a personal interview. This enables the faculty, who are members of the Admissions Committee, to become better acquainted with the student and thereafter to offer advice on a more personal and intimate basis. The catalogs of the seminaries provide detailed information as to admissions procedures and special requirements. For example, the HUC–JIR now requires that applicants to its Rabbinic School take the Graduate Record Examination (GRE).

If you live in the metropolitan centers where the seminaries are located, or you attend a college or university that offers instruction in Hebraica and Jewish studies, it will usually be possible for you to take courses in Hebrew language and literature and other subjects in Judaica. This will lead to better preparation for the ensuing more difficult studies, as well as advanced placement. If you live outside such a locale, study with an alumnus or with a tutor is recommended after you have been informed of specific requirements for admission.

We are now ready to explore the specific requirements of admission, courses of study, scholarships and grants-in-aid, residence facilities, scholarly resources, and employment for the rabbinical student.

VARIETIES OF JEWISH LEARNING

Hebrew Union College–Jewish Institute of Religion (Reform)
History and Program. The Hebrew Union College–Jewish Institute of Religion is America's oldest Jewish seminary with a continuous history. It was founded in 1875 by the architect

of American Reform Judaism, Rabbi Isaac Mayer Wise. The Jewish Institute of Religion was established in New York by Rabbi Stephen S. Wise in 1922. Under the presidency of Rabbi Nelson Glueck, the two schools were merged in 1950. A third center of rabbinic training was developed in 1954 in the fastest-growing Jewish community in America when the Los Angeles School of the HUC–JIR was chartered. In 1963 a postdoctoral research center was opened in Jerusalem, now known as the Nelson Glueck School of Biblical Archaeology. In a preface to the most recent catalog, I described our institution as follows:

> Hebrew Union College–Jewish Institute of Religion is the institution of higher learning in American Reform Judaism. It is dedicated to the study of Judaism and related areas in the spirit of free inquiry. Nothing in the Jewish or general past or present is alien to our interest. Sensitive to the challenge imposed on us by a world of change, we believe that Jewish ideas and values, along with the contributions of other religions and civilizations, are meaningful to the building of the future.
>
> We welcome students who meet the high standards of scholarship for which the College–Institute is known and who are committed to academic excellence and to serving the Jewish people and humankind.

Upon returning from the required year of Hebraic study at the Jerusalem campus, students continue their studies at one of the three stateside campuses of the College–Institute. The rabbinic schools in Cincinnati and New York offer the remaining four-year curriculum. The California school offers the first two years, leading to the Master of Arts in Hebrew Letters (M.A.H.L.); thereafter, the student transfers to either Cincinnati or New York to complete the academic program.

Facilities. The New York and Los Angeles campuses do not have dormitory facilities. In Cincinnati, dormitory, recreational, and dining facilities exist. The combined libraries of the four campuses represent one of the great collections of Judaica in the world. The Klau library in Cincinnati contains over 330,000 printed volumes and more than 2,000 manuscript codices. The American Jewish Archives and the American Jewish Periodical Center constitute major research facilities in the field of American Jewish history. The Archives now has approximately 8,000,000 pages of documents. The Skirball Museum, presently housed in the Los Angeles School, has a rich collection of Jewish art and artifacts. The New York School library contains 115,000 volumes and is especially strong in modern Hebrew literature. The Los Angeles campus library has a well-rounded Judaica collection of 70,000 volumes with a strong emphasis on Jewish education and communal service. The Biblical Archaeology School in Jerusalem is primarily a postdoctoral research institution, and also offers a Judaic Studies program for the training of Progressive Rabbis for Israel. A unique Reform service in Hebrew is conducted in the Jerusalem School's chapel.

Tuition, Scholarships, Bursary Aid. The tuition fee for graduate rabbinic students is $5,100 annually. The fee for residence at the Cincinnati dormitory is $2,800 for the academic year. In addition, a modest hygiene health fee is required on all campuses, including medical and hospitalization plans. Bursary aid is available in the form of deferred tuition, cash grants, or scholarships. No worthy student in need has ever been denied the opportunity to complete his or her rabbinic study because of insufficiency of funds.

Course of Study. HUC–JIR's program of rabbinic studies mandates a Year-in-Israel program for all first-year students. This program, which employs the Ulpan method of Hebrew instruction, concentrates on developing proficiency in modern Hebrew. It is also designed to deepen the student's understanding of the land, the people, and the institutions of Israel.

During the second through fifth years of study, students are offered a vast array of courses ranging from Akkadian, Arabic, Syriac, Ugaritic, and Greek to Hebrew language, Bible, Liturgy, Jewish Philosophy, Jewish Theology, Talmud and Commentaries, Midrash, and Homiletics. Extensive courses are provided in Jewish History and in the general field of Hebrew Literature. Candidates for the rabbinate also take courses in Human Relations, Jewish Education, and Speech. A host of electives is available for upper-class students in addition to specialized preparation for writing their rabbinic theses.

Field Training. During the student's years of study, many types of opportunity exist for earning a living. Although these are necessarily of a part-time nature, they range from religious school teaching, youth group direction, or private tutoring to weekly and biweekly rabbinic assignments in the cluster of communitites that surround the college campuses. Such employment opportunities are viewed by HUC–JIR as training situations, and the student rabbinic positions are closely supervised by members of the faculty, who act as counselors.

If your interest is in the Reform rabbinate, the Hebrew Union College–Jewish Institute of Religion is the place for you.

Reconstructionist Rabbinical College (RRC)

History and Program. The Reconstructionist Rabbinical College is a graduate institution dedicated to the training of rabbis for service in every area of the North American Jewish community. Established in Philadelphia in 1968 under the leadership of its President Emeritus Dr. Ira Eisenstein, the RRC had, as of 1985, graduated over eighty rabbis. These rabbis serve in a variety of leadership positions throughout the Jewish community: RRC graduates may serve in a synagogue, teach in a university, act as a resource person for a network of *havurot*, work with a Jewish federation, direct a Hillel foundation, or staff a Jewish communal agency. RRC students are exposed to the widest possible range of roles, from which they eventually will choose—and in some cases create—those that best reflect their own interest.

The five-year program of the RRC, and indeed the fundamental perspectives of Reconstructionist Judaism, derive from the teachings of Rabbi Mordecai M. Kaplan.

Reconstructionism defines Judaism as the evolving religious civilization of the Jewish people. Accordingly, Judaism has passed through distinct stages, each reflecting the conditions under which it functioned. At RRC, therefore, students concentrate each year on a specific period of Jewish history —Biblical, Rabbinic, Medieval, Modern, and Contemporary —through a series of courses dealing with the history, thought, and literature of each period. (Applicants who are otherwise qualified but whose knowledge of Hebrew is below standard are required to take a Preparatory Year program.)

Facilities. In 1982 the RRC moved to its new home and campus in suburban Wyncote, Pennsylvania, just north of the Philadelphia city line. A red brick slate-roofed Georgian mansion, the main building houses the Mordecai M. Kaplan Library and Archives, a chapel, classrooms and seminar rooms, faculty and administrative offices, and a student lounge and dining hall.

No dormitory facilities are provided at the RRC; the majority of students live in apartments and houses within driving distance of the College.

Tuition, Scholarships, Bursary Aid. Tuition is $4,000 annually. A limited number of scholarships are available and are awarded by the Admissions Committee. The RRC Board of Governors maintains a committee to deal with requests for additional financial aid and adjustments. The College is committed to creating financial arrangements for any student who requires them to matriculate and/or complete his/her course of study.

Field Training. Preparation for the practical rabbinate is offered through courses in pastoral counseling, education, and other rabbinic skills. In the final two years of the program, students declare a major area of study and take advanced courses in that area, enabling them to prepare in depth those areas of Judaica that they see as central to their own rabbinate.

In the Philadelphia Jewish community, students gain professional experience and fulfill community service requirements through supervised in-service training in synagogues, agencies, and schools.

All RRC students are required to spend an equivalency year of study in Israel. The Israel year is normally taken during the second, third, or fourth year of the program. The RRC believes that rabbinic students benefit most from an active involvement in Israeli academic and religious life. Consequently, RRC students study at Hebrew University and other approved institutions in Israel. The College staff includes two coordinators of Israel programs (dealing with academic and personal issues) resident in Jerusalem.

In keeping with the conviction that rabbis need to have a firm understanding of the world in which they serve, the RRC curriculum includes required study in world religions, the social sciences, and philosophy, emphasizing those areas in each field that interact with and influence Judaism throughout its historical development.

Upon successful completion of the program, students receive the title of rabbi and the Master of Arts in Hebrew Letters.

Jewish Theological Seminary of America (Conservative)
History and Program. The Jewish Theological Seminary of America is the Conservative movement's rabbinical training center, located in New York City. Chartered in 1886, it was the inspired instrument of Dr. Sabato Morais. Its present chancellor, Dr. Ismar Schorsch, is an outstanding scholar and administrator. The Seminary, which has as its motto "The preservation in America of the knowledge and practice of historical Judaism...," was shaped to this image by past president Dr. Solomon Schechter, who became famous as the discoverer of the Cairo Genizah, a cache of thousands of ancient manuscripts that filled many lacunae in the knowledge of Jewish letters.

Dr. Schechter was committed to the ideal of "traditional yet scientific Jewish scholarship." He held that:

> Judaism must stand or fall by that which distinguishes it from other religions as well as by that which it has in common with them ... There is no other Jewish religion but that taught by the Torah and confirmed by history and

tradition, and sunk into the conscience of catholic Israel
. . . .

This theological position, articulated during Schechter's presidency (1902–1915), still animates the Seminary today. The Seminary's Rabbinical School is a graduate-level professional school training men and women for the rabbinate. Applicants must have completed their undergraduate education at an accredited liberal arts college. If deemed qualified, they enter a six-year program toward ordination. Those who enter with considerable background in Judaica may complete the course requirements leading to ordination in less than six years.

The Seminary states as a requirement for admission to the rabbinical department that a student must be a member of the Jewish faith, conduct his or her life according to Jewish law and tradition, have high moral standards, and be observant of the Sabbath, festivals, daily prayers, and dietary laws.

The Seminary recommends the following courses as being helpful to students who are planning to enter the rabbinical department: English literature and composition; German or French; Latin or Greek; ancient, medieval, and modern history; philosophy, social sciences, and psychology.

Applicants are required to take standardized aptitude tests, to undergo preliminary interviews with the Dean, and finally, to be interviewed by the entire Admissions Committee. A Hebrew placement examination is also administered; it tests the knowledge of Hebrew grammar and the ability to read and translate unpointed Hebrew texts, and requires the candidate to write a Hebrew composition and to converse in simple Hebrew.

Facilities. The Seminary's facilities provide two dormitories. Its library of over 250,000 volumes and 10,000 manuscripts is considered one of the largest collections of Judaica ever assembled. The Seminary also sponsors an outstanding Jewish Museum with a valuable collection of ritual and art objects.

Tuition, Scholarships, Bursary Aid. Tuition in the Rabbinical School is $4,400 for the academic year; dormi-

tory fees range from $1,300 to $2,150. The Seminary provides scholarships to students by application and upon demonstration of need.
Course of Study. The curriculum focuses on Hebrew, Bible, Talmud, Midrash, and Codes, as well as on Jewish history, philosophy, and literature. The Seminary also requires courses in professional areas, such as homiletics, education, practical theology, and pastoral psychology. The curriculum is graded so as to correspond to a student's growth in his or her studies.
Field Training. The Jewish Theological Seminary has an internship program in which cooperating rabbis aid in the training of students in the day-to-day work of the rabbinate. This is generally done within two or three years of ordination. Students are assigned to assist a rabbi, with whom they must conduct evaluation sessions of their work. Alternatively, they work in hospitals, military chaplaincy training, or educational institutions.

Rabbi Isaac Elchanan Theological Seminary (Orthodox)

History and Program. The Rabbi Isaac Elchanan Theological Seminary (RIETS) is described as "the leading school in the nation for the training of Orthodox rabbis." The school, which was the hub out of which Yeshiva University developed, evolved from two of the oldest *yeshivot* in the nation: Yeshiva Eitz Hayim, founded in 1886, and the Rabbi Isaac Elchanan Theological Seminary, founded ten years later for the specific purpose of providing intensive study in Talmud. The new Yeshiva was named in honor of Rabbi Isaac Elchanan Spektor of Kovno (1817–1896), one of the outstanding rabbinical figures of his generation who was famous for his Responsa, which were original in the new principles of legal interpretation that they espoused.
Yeshiva University, which today embraces several colleges and schools, has as its president Rabbi Norman Lamm, a brilliant and distinguished figure in Jewish religious life. Rabbi Lamm has stated:

A good part of the functioning of a rabbi, in the many aspects of his career as a teacher of Torah and leader of his community, depends upon his self-confidence—a psychological and also spiritual issue which involves his self-image as a rabbi and student of Torah, and his conception of his role, his identity, and his destiny.

The late Rabbi Samuel Belkin (1911–1976), Dr. Lamm's predecessor, observed that, "traditionally and spiritually, the University is strengthened by those unique characteristics that it has inherited from the *yeshivot*—a sacred regard for knowledge and a devotion to the high moral and ethical values of Judaism." The RIETS is modeled after traditional *yeshivot*. Torah is studied intensively, with great emphasis placed upon the Talmud, Responsa literature, and the *Shulhan Arukh*. The RIETS also trains rabbis who choose to be scholars, teachers, religious educators, and cantors.

Facilities. The RIETS is located in New York City, and offers housing to single graduate students. The Seminary has an excellent library in Judaica and Hebraica, which is incorporated into the central Yeshiva University library designed to house more than one million volumes.

Tuition, Scholarships, Bursary Aid. Tuition and fees are so structured that students who attend the *semikhah* program pay only a registration fee of $150. A *semikhah* fellowship program aids gifted students, enabling them to devote full time to their rabbinic studies. Unmarried students may receive up to $1,900 and free dormitory housing for the academic year; married students may receive up to $4,000.

Course of Study. At RIETS, *semikhah* represents "the oral or written conferral of rabbinical authority. It certifies that a man has qualified as a rabbi by virtue of intensive knowledge of the Talmud, *halakhah* (codes) and his exemplary personal piety." He is presumed to be a master of both the oral and written traditions of Jewish law and lore.

The course of study has recently been extended from a three-year to a four-year postgraduate academic program.

Students entering the *semikhah* program have usually engaged in intensive Jewish studies for at least eight years before admission. Since the *semikhah* curriculum stresses the study of Talmud, students bring with them a Jewish day school background and have studied Talmud for a year or two at an advanced yeshivah in Israel. Nevertheless, it is not uncommon for young men without this background to prepare themselves, with diligence and study, to enter the *semikhah* program at RIETS. Such students should consult with RIETS admissions officers to obtain appropriate guidance and counsel.

Rabbi Zevulun Charlap, Director of the RIETS *semikhah* program, characterizes the curriculum as follows:

> RIETS' approach to curriculum is hardly distinguishable from the classical *yeshivah*. Its chief goal is also to prepare *talmidei hakhamim* (scholars), and it allows its students to pursue Torah studies in much the same way as any other yeshivah. There are, however, several critical differences that give it a *persona* all its own: 1) the acceptance of secular learning, although it should be noted that in the *semikhah* program proper there is no secular intrusion; 2) its relation to the outside world and particularly to Zionism and the State of Israel; 3) its aggressive commitment to the totality of the Jewish people.

The *semikhah* program at RIETS also requires that a student select an academic concentration to supplement his core work in Talmud and codes. These programs include: a) six semesters of study in the Department of Jewish Thought; b) completing an M.A. or M.S. at the Bernard Revel Graduate School; c) completing an M.S. in Jewish Education at the Ferkauf Graduate School; d) completing an M.S.W. at the Wurzweiler School of Social Work.

A student may elect to substitute the *Kollel* program for the concentrations noted above. The Katz Kollel (Institute for Advanced Research in Rabbinics) offers *semikhah* and post-*semikhah* students an intensified program in Talmud and

Rabbinic codes and is for students planning to make a career of teaching Talmud.

Field Training. The candidate for the Orthodox rabbinate also has much opportunity for field training. Teaching and rabbinic training positions are available to RIETS students through the *Shimush*-Fieldwork program. A large variety of practical field experience is a required component of the *semikhah* program in the third and fourth years of study.

Other Jewish Seminaries

The Hebrew Union College-Jewish Institute of Religion, the Reconstructionist Rabbinical College, and the Jewish Theological Seminary are the only rabbinic training centers in America for the Reform, Reconstructionist, and Conservative movements, respectively.

In addition to Yeshiva University's RIETS, there are scores of Orthodox *yeshivot.* Foremost among them is the Hebrew Theological College of Skokie, Illinois; Yeshivat Torah Vodaath and Mesivta Rabbinical Seminary in Brooklyn, New York; the Beth Midrash Gevoha, Lakewood, New Jersey; Central Yeshive Tomchei T'mimim Lubavich, Brooklyn; Rabbi Jacob Joseph School and Mesivta, New York; Rabbinical College of Telshe, Cleveland, Ohio; and Rabbi Hayyim Berlin Rabbinical Academy, Brooklyn. These Orthodox *yeshivot* represent particular viewpoints within the spectrum of traditional Jewish thought, ranging from the hasidic to the anti-hasidic. Most of these *yeshivot* have their own alumni groupings and rabbinic associations. In these *yeshivot*, many students are pursuing rabbinic courses who may or may not choose to be ordained. This is true also of RIETS. It is not the case with the HUC–JIR, the RRC, or the JTS. The students who enroll in these seminaries seek to be ordained as rabbis and, upon graduation, wish to practice their profession.

OPPORTUNITY FOR STUDY IN ISRAEL

Today, the major seminaries provide their students with an opportunity to study in Israel. The HUC–JIR requires that all first-year rabbinic students enroll in the Year-in-Israel program, designed primarily to develop proficiency in modern Hebrew. During the program, students are required to undertake a service project while they study in Jerusalem to heighten their understanding of Israeli life and society.

The JTS maintains the American Student Center in Jerusalem, which provides residential quarters, classrooms, and a library for students of the Rabbinical School doing their required year of study in Israel. The Seminary maintains both full-time and part-time faculty members, an academic dean, and a student adviser.

Yeshiva University maintains the Gruss Israel Institute in Jerusalem. According to the RIETS catalogue, "the Gruss Institute, opened in 1977, offers pre-*semikhah*, *semikhah*, and post-*semikhah* programs, the last of which gives students the opportunity to pursue advanced research or, through work with such bodies as rabbinic courts of law, gain experience in traditional rabbinic practice. There is full reciprocity between the RIETS School in New York and that in Jerusalem."

All branches of American Judaism have established cultural centers in Israel for the purpose of creating a bridge between the two great centers of Jewish life. Most recently, HUC–JIR has embarked upon an ambitious expansion of its Jerusalem campus to enlarge its facility and dramatize the presence of Reform Judaism in Israel. Each of the movements attempts to relate the significance of its philosophy to Israel, and that of Israel to its adherents in the Diaspora.

NATIONAL AND INTERNATIONAL UNIONS OF JEWISH CONGREGATIONS

Each of the seminaries serves a constituency of congregations that have combined into voluntary associations. The Union of American Hebrew Congregations (1873) represents at this writing 791 Reform congregations in the United States and Canada. The UAHC is the patron of the HUC–JIR. Regional offices of the UAHC are in the major metropolitan centers of America. The Reform movement has a worldwide organization known as the World Union for Progressive

Judaism, which has 125 congregations outside of the U.S. and Canada associated with it. The HUC–JIR student may elect to serve one of these World Union congregations during his or her student years or after ordination.

The Federation of Reconstructionist Congregations and Havurot (1954) coordinates the policies and activities of Reconstructionist congregations and havurot. As of 1985, there were over fifty affiliated groups. Regional and national programs include lectures, workshops, retreats, intercongregational exchanges, an annual convention and youth *kallah*, and the creation of policy statements.

The United Synagogue of America (1913) is the national association of 850 Conservative congregations in the United States, Canada, and Mexico, with forty-two additional congregations in Israel. Its headquarters is in New York City, where numerous commissions and departments carry out the stated programs of the Conservative movement on a congregational basis, also serving its regional offices in major cities throughout North America. In 1957 the USA formed the World Council of Synagogues, which represents fifteen countries throughout the world. In 1959 a prerabbinic educational program was started for the regional office of the World Council of Synagogues in Buenos Aires, offering the preliminary courses leading to admission by the School of Judaica of the JTS.

The Union of Orthodox Jewish Congregations of America (1898) is the central body of Orthodox synagogues. One of its chief functions is to conduct a national Kashruth certification service, in addition to carrying out the avowed program of the traditional community of America. The UOJC has not revealed the number of its member congregations, since the definition of membership is somewhat hazy. At various times the UOJC had claimed to serve as many as 3,100 congregations. A more realistic estimate would indicate that of the 1,700 synagogues that call themselves Orthodox, only a portion could possibly be affiliated with the UOJC. The Orthodox community has no centrally organized world movement. There are, however, a number of sectarian

Orthodox groupings that function on a worldwide scale. Among them are the Agudath Israel, which was founded in Europe in 1912 and organized in the United States in 1929; and the Hasidic Lubavitcher movement, followers of the Lubavitcher rabbi. There are other hasidic groupings that have a worldwide following, although their collective numbers are not readily available.

RABBINICAL ORGANIZATIONS

When the seminarian has completed a required course of study and is ordained, the new colleague is welcomed by the rabbinic organization of his or her particular movement. In the Reform movement this is the Central Conference of American Rabbis (1889). It has a membership of nearly 1,500 rabbis, most of whom were ordained at the HUC–JIR or a comparable liberal seminary in Europe. The CCAR also has an alumni association, which supports specific publications of the HUC–JIR and other worthwhile projects. The CCAR meets annually and, through its resolutions, addresses itself to problems of world Jewry, war and peace, social and economic equality, and a host of other issues related to the interpretation of liberal Judaism on the American scene.

The Reconstructionist Rabbinical Association (1975) is composed of graduates of the RRC as well as graduates of other rabbinical programs who choose to identify with Reconstructionist Judaism. Numbering over 100 rabbis, the Association meets annually in convention, maintains committees that address specific rabbinic concerns, and participates in joint commissions with the Federation of Reconstructionist Congregations and Havurot in addressing issues of mutual concern to Reconstructionist laity and rabbis. The Association maintains an office at the RRC.

The Rabbinical Assembly (1901) is an international association of over 1,180 Conservative rabbis. It, too, convenes an annual assembly and seeks to implement the programs and ideologies of Conservative Judaism. The RA's constitution specifies that its purpose is:

... To ... promote Conservative Judaism; to cooperate with the Jewish Theological Seminary of America and with United Synagogue of America; to advance the cause of Jewish learning; to promote the welfare of the members; and to foster the spirit of fellowship and cooperation among the rabbis and other Jewish scholars.

The Rabbinical Council of America (1923, reorganized 1935) is the largest and most influential association of Orthodox rabbis in the United States. Of its 1,000 members, about 600 are estimated to be in the active rabbinate, the rest being religious school administrators and teachers. The RCA meets annually and, like the CCAR and the RA, issues statements on the policy of the movement and on matters that are relevant to Jewish life. The members of the RCA are, for the most part, rabbis ordained at the Rabbi Isaac Elchanan Theological Seminary and the Hebrew Theological College of Skokie, Illinois. The remaining RCA membership is derived from graduates of other American and European *yeshivot*.

The various rabbinic associations have created a host of commissions to deal with the day-to-day work of developing their respective movements. The Reform, Conservative, and Orthodox rabbinic bodies publish the authorized prayerbooks, special liturgies, and religious tracts for their movements. They also publish *Year Books* containing the proceedings of their annual conventions, as well as quarterly journals containing articles, sermons, and various other types of studies relating to the problems of Jewish life in America and the world. From the three major rabbinic organizations, chaplains are secured for the armed services. The associations also participate in or sponsor rabbinic placement offices through which rabbis apply for new pulpits and changes in pulpits. The various rabbinic organizations contain on their rosters some of the greatest rabbis of America and the world. They are formidable in advancing the interests of the rabbinate in America.

Chapter IV

Ordained For Service

SELECTING A FIELD OF SERVICE

The ordination ceremony, which marks the culmination of the rabbinic candidate's many years of study and training, inaugurates a lifetime of service to the Jewish people. His or her previous preparation through biweekly assignments, Hebrew teaching, a year abroad, or possibly an internship, all have aided the new rabbi's growth and development. Often, the experiences of these formative student years shape a life's work in a given direction. A student may have been found to possess considerable gifts as a preacher, another may have found people responsive in counseling situations, and still another may have enjoyed the varied contacts of active Jewish communal life. Some find themselves proficient as teachers, and others have a capacity for deep and ongoing scholarship. At ordination time, the rabbinic student begins to ask the fundamental questions as to the meaning of his or her impending rabbinate and, depending upon how those questions are answered, seeks certain types of opportunities.

Graduating rabbinic students normally find their work through a placement process. Rabbis already in the field, as well as those returning from chaplaincy duties, also seek new positions. They turn to the various rabbinic placement services, each of which has its own set of procedures and requirements. Within each movement a sophisticated code of ethics prevails, the breach of which jeopardizes the future placement of a rabbi.

The Max Stern Division of Community Services at RIETS publishes a pamphlet entitled "Procedures and Policy for Rabbinic Placement." *Musmachim* (ordinees) of RIETS are served by the placement board of the Division of Community Services (DCS) from the moment they enter the *semikhah* program. The services of DCS are also available to all members of the Rabbinical Council of America, which does not maintain its own placement office. To qualify for placement, it is necessary to register with the DCS, which functions as a liaison between the community and rabbis seeking a post. The DCS also directs the placement of rabbis in noncongregational positions such as organizational, Hillel, and educational posts.

The Joint Commission on Rabbinic Placement, under the auspices of the Jewish Theological Seminary of America, the Rabbinical Assembly of America, and the United Synagogue of America, processes Conservative rabbis seeking placement. The Joint Commission considers itself guided by the following considerations: (a) requirements of the congregation, (b) qualifications of the candidates, (c) seniority of candidate, (d) chaplaincy service, and (e) needs of candidates.

The Rabbinical Placement Commission of the Reform movement is a joint commission also, representing the CCAR, the UAHC, and the HUC–JIR. This commission has published guidelines on rabbinic placement for both rabbis and congregations. It is the position of the Reform Commission that "a rabbi will not be considered for a change of position until he or she has been in a post long enough to have achieved some useful results." The Reform movement bases its placement on the size of the congregation, the length of service and experience of the rabbi, and additional guidelines for various situations and complexities that may arise. The Commission's placement procedures are absolutely binding on members of the CCAR.

Normally, placement procedure operates as follows: Upon

the retirement, resignation, or dismissal of an incumbent rabbi, a placement commission declares a given pulpit to be vacant. It then officially informs the members of its affiliated rabbinic organization of the nature of the congregation and the categories of rabbis who are eligible to apply for the pulpit. A panel of names is drawn up, derived from suggestions originating from within the congregation, recommendations by other rabbis, and the placement commission. The first panel, which may consist of ten to twelve names, is submitted to the congregation, which chooses to interview one or as many of the rabbis as it feels qualify for its pulpit. The decision is then made by both the rabbis interviewed and the congregation to accept or reject the pulpit offer.

The interview procedures, although standarized by the rabbinic placement commissions, realistically vary with the congregation, since each congregation is autonomous. Each congregation naturally attempts to find the rabbinic candidate best suited to its particular needs. Among matters that are discussed in the interview are the rabbi's theological views and their compatibility with those of the preponderant number of congregants, the scope of his or her responsibilities to the congregation and community, salary, pension provisions, and emoluments or other benefits, such as housing, that the congregation may be willing to provide.

If the rabbi is interviewing for a first pulpit, either as an assistant or as the spiritual leader of a smaller congregation, the salary offered is probably in the vicinity of other professionals with four or more years of post graduate study. For a Hillel Foundation directorship, the beginning salary would be approximately the same. Another benefit the congregational rabbi receives is a parsonage allowance, which is legally deductible from income for tax purposes and which is used to maintain a home.

As the rabbi grows in the profession and gains stature and recognition, he or she may choose to leave a situation, having successfully met its challenge, for yet more responsible obligations. At this juncture, a rabbi again turns to the rabbinic placement commission of his or her movement and applies for congregations that offer advancement and a greater opportunity for service.

CAREER OPPORTUNITIES

The Military Chaplaincy

Service to men and women in the armed forces is an important option for rabbinic work. Since the clergy, by law, cannot be drafted, it has required the inner discipline of the main branches of American Judaism to provide the armed forces with a sufficient number of Jewish chaplains to minister to the needs of Jewish military personnel. World War II, particularly, made of the chaplaincy a moral and patriotic commitment on the part of the rabbinate. The late Rabbi Bertram Korn, commemorating the centennial of the Jewish chaplaincy of the United States, wrote of the fascinating Reverend Jacob Frankel, cantor of Rodef Sholom Congregation of Philadelphia, who in 1862 "achieved the distinction of becoming the first Jewish chaplain to be commissioned by the American government, or by any government for that matter, for ministration to Jews in the uniform of their country."

Since World War I, the Jewish Welfare Board (JWB) has been recognized by the American government as the agency that provides "religious and moral services to the Jewish military personnel and veteran hospital patients." The JWB Commission on Jewish Chaplaincy recruits, helps to train, and provides a religious support system for Jewish chaplains and Jewish personnel in the armed forces and the Veterans Administration. It furnishes them with religious supplies, literature, and program aids. When World War II broke out, a Committee on Army, Navy, and Religious Activities of JWB was organized, which included representatives of the three largest religious movements. The Commission on Jewish Chaplaincy was composed, until recently, of seven rabbis designated by each of the three major rabbinical organizations, the CCAR, the RA, and the RCA. In 1986 the Commission was reorganized in response to the introduction of women into the military chaplaincy. The successor body, the Jewish Chaplains Council, is composed of four delegates from each of the three rabbinic organizations.

Formerly, most chaplains served on active duty for a period of two or three years. Today, chaplaincy is frequently a permanent career. The Jewish Chaplains Council–JWB has more than fifty chaplains on active duty, most of whom have chosen the chaplaincy as a career. More than 40 percent are members of the CCAR. Upon completion of twenty to thirty years of military service, chaplains may retire and receive a life pension of $20,000 to $32,000. Men and women are always needed for the chaplaincy. The CCAR is empowered by the Department of Defense–Armed Forces Chaplains Board to endorse qualified Reform rabbis, men and women, to serve as chaplains. As military preparedness continues to be part of the program of our country, the need for chaplains will remain.

During World War II it was estimated that about half the eligible rabbis of the United States volunteered for chaplaincy service. Of those who applied, 422 received endorsement and 311 actually served. During those years, Jewish chaplains played a heroic role in aiding the victims of Nazi oppression. They performed miraculous acts of deliverance in helping to set up the necessary social agencies for the survivors of the concentration camps. They performed many acts of mercy and assisted survivors who wished to leave Europe to go to Israel and other lands. Perhaps the dedication of the chaplaincy may best be illustrated by the bravery of "The Four Chaplains," one of whom was Rabbi Alexander D. Goode. The Four Chaplains were on duty on the transport *Dorchester* in the North Atlantic when the ship was struck by a torpedo. The chaplains gave their life jackets to members of the ship's crew, as there was a shortage, giving up their own lives for others. As the vessel was sinking, a last view of the chaplains found them standing at the ship's rail deeply engrossed in prayer.

The list of rabbis on the roster of organizations working for peace throughout the world is as long as the rabbis' voices have been vigorous. Yet when war occurs, they have responded to help those in the front lines of the conflict. Chaplain Edward T. Sandrow (1906–1975) wrote from Alaska during World War II:

Never in my life have I seen men so eager for spiritual expression as I have found them here . . . Restlessness and intense activity do not deter them from religious fellowship . . . Wherever I have gone, hungry men have literally lapped whatever drops of spiritual nourishment I could give them. Religion is a matter of tremendous concern to these men. The power of faith—our faith—is the answer. I can better understand our history now. Backgrounds dissolve; the same thirst and yearning for God remains.

The Jewish chaplain represents the value system of Judaism to those in service to our country. The chaplain is a confidant, friend, and, most important, a link to home and family. By virtue of this role, the Jewish chaplain has been an interpreter of Judaism to large numbers of non-Jews. A chaplain must also be ready to minister to the needs of persons of other faiths. As part of the daily work, the chaplain conducts services and ceremonies, cares for the sick and wounded, buries the dead, and teaches and counsels the soldier in uniform.

Rabbi Hillel E. Silverman summarized the vital role of the Jewish military chaplain when he wrote this recollection of his own days as a chaplain:

As a chaplain, you are not selling religion, not merchandising Judaism. Religion is not a commodity. You don't have to look for people to attend services. They seek you out. They want you. They need you. They want to talk to you, want your help with their problems.

In the military, there is no denominationalism. . . The noun, Jew, is far more important than the adjective Orthodox, Conservative, or Reform.

The Pulpit Rabbi

By far the largest number of rabbis who are active in their field occupy pulpits. The pulpit rabbinate is one of the most challenging, rewarding, and complex of professions. The rabbi is elected by a congregation or its board to serve them. Rabbi Emanuel Rose observed that the rabbi's

... rights and obligations do not derive from the congregation ... A rabbi must feel strength and security not in the numbers (although they are very comforting to be sure) who agree, but in a deep belief in and commitment to the ethical validity of his [or her] position.

The rabbi voices with conviction the sense of values that is conceived to be his or her mandate in the teaching of the Jewish people. A strong rabbi directs the religious affairs of a congregation with vision and courage and is prepared for frustration and opposition. For, if all Jews were prophets, there would hardly be a need for the rabbi or the rabbinate.

Because Jewish congregations are highly individualistic and because Judaism lacks a religious hierarchy, the rabbi's success depends upon his or her talents as a persuader. The story is told of a rabbi and a priest discussing their respective difficulties. The priest said to the rabbi, "I can't tell you how difficult it is to be a priest of a parish of 500 Catholic communicants," to which the rabbi replied, "And you can't imagine how difficult it is to be the rabbi of a congregation of 500 rabbis." The rough-and-tumble of the democratic process is nowhere as evident as in congregational life. It is no longer possible even for the the Orthodox rabbi to take refuge in tradition alone; he, too, is often subject to the challenge and consensus of the congregation. The modern rabbi must remain relevant and talk in the language of the congregants.

The congregational rabbi's work is mostly with members of the congregation. Normally, the rabbi supervises the religious school and may or may not be the actual principal of that school. The rabbi teaches the confirmation class, develops and participates in adult education programs, and directs the religious affairs of the auxiliary groups of the temple, men's and women's clubs, youth groups, and allied boards. Foremost among the rabbi's obligations is that of religious leader in public worship, fearlessly preaching the mandates of Judaism, ministering to the sick and the bereaved, and counseling those who are troubled. There are many more community obligations that have already been delineated. The congregational rabbi must be a person of great energy and vision, who can meaningfully conduct congregational affairs.

At the Central Conference of American Rabbis convention in 1963, a rare symposium took place between Rabbi Solomon B. Freehof of Pittsburgh and Rabbi Abba Hillel Silver of Cleveland. Both men had made exceptional careers in the pulpit. In the symposium, the rabbis asked one another about the standards of success and failure in their rabbinates. In response to Rabbi Freehof's question, "What should be the prime function of a rabbi?" Dr. Silver replied,

I know that many other duties are demanded of the modern rabbi, many of which one must perform—pastor to the flock, tribune of the Jewish people to the non-Jewish world, defender of social justice and human rights. But principally, in my humble judgment, the rabbi, as the name signifies, is teacher—not pastor, but teacher. By teaching young and old the spiritual and ethical documents of Judaism, and thereby inspiring in them a life of personal integrity and social responsibility, the rabbi makes a major contribution to individual communicants, to the congregation, and to the community.

I know that is not a sensational answer; that's the answer I can give you.

Rabbi Silver then asked Rabbi Freehof about success in the rabbinate, to which the rabbi replied, "I would count the rabbi's success by how many people he [or she] trains to divine worship. Now, this may be an outward sign, but it also may be what the Episcopalians call the 'outer visible sign of an inner invisible quest.'" Rabbi Silver asked what was the greatest obstacle in a rabbi's career, to which Rabbi Freehof replied,

> The rabbi's own inherent deficiencies. If a rabbi lacks character or courage or tact or sensitivity, a career is likely to be destroyed.
>
> If one's heart is set on false objectives, in quest of excessive publicity—we all like a certain amount of publicity—or on being well-liked by everybody, or on never saying anything that will not be approved by everybody, that rabbi will corrode from within, in the long run.

Rabbi Silver also pointed to other obstacles that rabbis encounter: the inertia of people, the sluggishness of progress, and downright opposition. But "these will not destroy or even retard one's true career. They will temper, strengthen, and help the rabbi's career to be fulfilled." No better advice could be given to those who aspire to prominence in the pulpit. Certainly, obstacles and frustrations are inevitable in the rabbinate, but so are its great and irreplaceable moments of triumph and achievement.

The Assistant and Associate Rabbi

In larger congregations the rabbi often requires an assistant. The assistant is usually a recent graduate of a seminary who has chosen to serve under the tutelage of a more experienced rabbi. Normally, the assistant has specific charge of the educational program of the synagogue or temple and assists the rabbi in many duties. The assistant is not a runner of errands but a colleague who has chosen an apprenticeship to learn the rabbinic craft from an experienced rabbi. Graduates generally gravitate toward a senior colleague whose rabbinate reflects their own values and from whom a great deal can be learned.

An assistantship may sometimes grow into an associate-ship, in which case rabbinic duties are shared equally. In larger congregations with more than one assistant, certain aspects of the work may be distributed so that the senior rabbi preaches and the educational and pastoral work is assigned to the assistants. There is much variation within congregations, depending upon the inclinations and talents of the rabbis. An assistantship/associateship lasts, on the average, for three to five years. The young rabbi then usually assumes a position of greater responsibility.

The Rabbi as College Professor

There has been a growing trend to establish chairs of Hebrew language and literature and of Judaica at large metropolitan campuses where a sizeable number of Jewish students are enrolled. It has been estimated that over 300 colleges and universities currently offer courses in Judaica and Hebraica. A modest increase in this trend is expected for the future. The seminaries that have grown in the past decade also need additional teachers. There have always been rabbis who were college professors, not a few of whom became distinguished scholars.

Scores of other rabbis engage in part-time teaching at seminaries, Jewish and Christian, and at universities. The directors of Hillel Foundations, in particular, are called upon to teach courses in Bible or Jewish Religious Thought on the campuses at which they serve. Numerous rabbis have earned doctorates in Hebrew letters or philosophy and thereby hold the proper credentials for appointment to professorial posts. This is an exciting new development on the American Jewish scene and provides an excellent opportunity for men and women who want to devote their entire energies to teaching and research.

The Rabbi as Hillel Director

The Hillel Foundation has long offered a unique opportunity for the rabbi interested in teaching, counseling, and programming with college-age youth and university faculty. Hillel work is immensely satisfying to rabbis who thrive in an intellectual, pluralistic, and interfaith atmosphere. For six decades, B'nai B'rith Hillel Foundations have functioned as the Jewish community's central address on campus. During those years, Hillel has grown from one foundation serving a few hundred students at the University of Illinois into a network spanning the North American continent, Europe, Israel, Australia, and South Africa. Hillel now reaches over 400 campuses with more than 430,000 Jewish students. Nearly 100 Foundations are guided by full-time Directors, often in multistaff operations. The remaining campuses are served by outreach workers, educators, part-time congregational rabbis, or communal service workers. In addition, a number of regional directors supervise given geographic areas. The first Hillel Foundation was founded by Rabbi Benjamin Frankel, a graduate of the College–Institute in 1923.

The Hillel Foundations maintain three chairs of Judaic studies: the Hillel professorship of Jewish Thought and Literature at Vanderbilt University, the Hillel professorship of Jewish Studies at the State University of Iowa, and the Hillel professorship of Hebrew Studies at the School of Religion of the University of Missouri.

Hillel is the Jewish presence on the college campus. Much as the myriad Jewish agencies meet the needs of a Jewish community, Hillel meets the social, cultural, religious, personal, and political needs of the college student. It is this many-faceted ministry that is Hillel's raison d'être. But, although some students will reach out to Hillel, the majority need to be reached by Hillel. It is in this effort that the challenge lies.

Dr. Alfred Jospe, former International Director of National Hillel, observed:

Specifically, the Hillel program encompasses activities which seek to provide Jewish students, through study and discussion, with adequate and accurate knowledge of Jewish life by acquainting them with the faith, the literature, the history and life and thought patterns of the Jewish people, which enable them to share in the religious and cultural Jewish expressions of the Jewish heritage with understanding and appreciation, and which will provide them with the opportunity to express their personality in activities aiming at the perpetuation and development of the Jewish religiocultural heritage.

The Hillel rabbi participates in the education and moral and religious development of Jewish college students in their most formative years; often the imprint that a Hillel rabbi leaves upon his or her students shapes their view of Judaism in their more mature years. As the senior Jewish professional and role model for young people age eighteen to twenty-five, the Hillel rabbi is in the forefront of fostering positive Jewish identification and the strengthening of Jewish communal and family values.

Historically, B'nai B'rith International has been the main funding source for all Hillels. Currently the majority of the Hillel units are funded in whole or in significant part by local and regional Jewish communities and federations. A national Hillel office is maintained in Washington, D.C. The national directors have as their primary responsibility governance, centralized administration, supervision, placement, and programming for the Hillel units. In addition, the concept of a national movement is maintained in the directors' professional association, the Association of Hillel and Jewish Campus Professionals (AHJCP). Salary scales are somewhat less than commensurate with congregational placements, but the "salary gap" has narrowed in recent years as Hillel boards increase their compensation in an effort to attract the best rabbinic candidates to the college campus. Opportunities often exist for Hillel rabbis to serve as lecturers on the campus.

The professional staff of the B'nai B'rith Hillel Foundations is covered by a full insurance program, which is funded by the organization and the participant. The coverage includes retirement insurance, life insurance, major medical plan, study leaves, and other benefits.

Rabbi Abie Ingber, a past president of the AHJCP, has written that "the (Hillel) movement is a rich and fertile soil for growth and development. The professional association is committed to nourishing the roots. Without the commitment to religious pluralism and the professional collegiality, Hillel work would be just a job—an important job—but just a job. Our *melachah*, our work, is central to the well-being of the American Jewish community."

The Nonmilitary Chaplaincy

A number of rabbis serve as chaplains in various types of institutions such as hospitals, mental institutions, prisons, homes for the aged, and orphanages. The work of the community chaplain may at times encompass most of these. In large metropolitan centers, the Jewish Federation Councils in conjunction with auxiliary agencies provide a chaplain whose task it is to bring religious programming and pastoral counseling to a wide variety of people in need. In addition to conducting services, such chaplains engage in counseling activities, ranging from helping to find work for a parolee to making a family cognizant of its responsibilities to one of its members who is institutionalized. The nonmilitary chaplain is virtually a social worker who, because of his or her talents as religious counselor and Jewish resource person, is engaged in a plethora of activities to bring help and comfort to people. Although many rabbis, particularly those in smaller communities, perform these functions as part of their regular congregational work, the full-time nonmilitary chaplaincy has developed into a highly specialized field.

Rabbi Samuel W. Chomsky has made himself expert as a Jewish chaplain in matters pertaining to veterans. Rabbi Chomsky, now a retired chaplain, points out that the Veterans Administration chaplain is primarily a hospital chaplain who works mostly with the acutely ill. He finds that counseling chronic and geriatric patients requires special skills to offset the fears and terrible loneliness of such victims. The VA chaplain also deals with mental patients, both young and old. Very often these people need ongoing encouragement to help them resume a normal life. To assist such patients, the chaplain uses different kinds of counseling skills, including religious services. It is vital to impart to these patients the feeling that someone cares deeply about them. Rabbi Chomsky observes, "An impersonal ministry would sometimes do more harm than no ministry at all." The chaplain, who represents the religious values of the Jewish tradition to these patients, has found that patients have a deeply felt need for prayer, since it relates to the concepts of faith, courage, hope, security, peace, and strength. Through prayer they feel the presence of God in their lives, and often this gives them the impetus to help themselves and to regain health of mind and body.

The Jewish chaplain in mental hospitals is a very important professional. Dr. Abraham N. Franzblau (1901–1982), in an address entitled "Functions of a Chaplain in a Mental Hospital," raised the question whether it is the function of the chaplain to administer therapy. Therapy can be viewed in either broad or strict terms. If one were to regard it as a skilled technique to be administered only by trained professionals, many chaplains would be excluded from therapy situations. However, therapy is a difficult term so to confine. All of its definitions imply helping to find a cure. Although some patients have mental illnesses that do not yet respond to treatment, there are, nevertheless, ways in which these people can be made more comfortable. Rabbis and candidates for rabbinic training who devote time to patients in mental hospitals often find themselves involved in therapy conferences. They report patients who yearn for someone to talk to, someone to respond to them. The mere proximity of another human being who was not institutionalized, who did not *have* to care, restored sparks of hope in patients who had well-nigh concluded that the outside world was not a whit affected whether they lived or died, whether they recovered or rotted away. Dr. Franzblau observed that the rabbi can do something important and unique in the life of a patient: The rabbi/chaplain can often assist in restoring the judgment of troubled persons and helping them to recover their sense of objectivity.

Unquestionably, rabbis who specialize as chaplains for

work in mental institutions must be trained in psychology, not only to understand their patients but also to understand themselves. However, if a rabbi is called upon to do extensive psychiatric counseling, there is no substitute for graduate work to become qualified as a clinical psychologist. A few rabbis have even gone on to study medicine and to become accredited as psychiatrists. In the profession of chaplain there is no room for amateurs. This is serious work involving the sanity and life of other human beings. The chaplain's training cannot be improvised or extemporaneous. Nothing can take the place of study and certification.

The chaplain who deals primarily with the emotionally and mentally disturbed must also have certain personal qualities. Rabbi Jerome Folkman observed, "Empathy is the basis of every counseling situation. The counselor must earn the right to counsel. And that privilege must be earned anew in each case." Unquestionably, it takes a special kind of human being to make a success of this highly complex career of ministering to the mentally ill.

The role of the correctional chaplain requires yet a different kind of specialization. Rabbi Iser L. Freund has pointed out that the office of the correctional chaplain was not orginally set up by the penal institutions themselves. In most cases ministers and representatives of religious organizations concerned with "the forgotten men in the jails ... worked themselves into the correctional system and brought solace, hope, and, sometimes, a little extra food to the imprisoned." Gradually, the correctional chaplaincy became a profession in which the chaplain performed more than just priestly duties in prison confines. Rabbi Freund maintained that the chaplain's "... functions and personality permeate the whole life of the prisoner and the prison community." While the chaplain preaches and teaches the principles of his or her faith, there is more:

> The chaplain is: the listener without a report; the conscience without chastisement; the sounding board for hostilities without disciplinary action; the eternal optimist

where despondency reigns; the chaplain walks around without a club and power; the chaplain looks at pictures of wives and children left behind; the chaplain is tolerant of sins without peeking into subterranean personality gutters; the chaplain rationalizes authority rather than enforces it; the chaplain listens (if wise, and most of them are) without interpretation; the chaplain is gullible without reprisal; the chaplain is soft in an environment where everything else is harsh; the chaplain is sympathetic even when one does not deserve it; the chaplain is a symbol of the family from which the prisoner is severed, and of the community from which the prisoner was separated or expelled; the chaplain is the liaison with the world outside, from which the prisoner is excluded and to which he or she passionately hopes to go back. The chaplain is high-minded and humble, reassuring that no life is worthless or completely depraved in the sight of God.

In this moving statement, Rabbi Freund brilliantly summarized the universal role of the rabbi, not just the chaplain in the correctional institution. Not very many rabbis seek this hard and challenging work as their vocation. Yet to serve the disinherited and the unwanted represents one of the highest callings in the Jewish faith. It is hoped that more rabbis can be secured for this immensely interesting and inwardly rewarding field.

The Rabbi as Executive Director
This catch-all description covers those who are essentially administrators. The national Jewish organizations such as congregational unions, B'nai B'rith, the American Jewish Committee, Zionist organizations, and a host of others may engage rabbis both on a national and regional level as program consultants or executives. Such work normally takes the rabbi out of congregational activity and propels him or her into organizational work, writing and editing journals and newspapers, fund-raising, organizing membership drives, public relations, and many other allied activities. One

might ask why it is necessary to be an ordained rabbi to do such work. The institutions engaging rabbis for these purposes would readily reply that the knowledge of Jewish tradition and history that the rabbi brings to the organization, as well as his or her normally superior intellectual qualities, are very valuable to them. The rabbi is a vital resource person who may have much influence in shaping the content and form of Jewish organizational life.

Although not an appreciable number of rabbis are engaged in this type of work, all indications are that the category is growing. As Jewish institutional life becomes more complex, more rabbis will become interested in affiliating with national and regional organizations. The satisfaction of the work for the rabbi comes from a clearly defined area of responsibility in a stable organizational structure and the opportunity of affecting large numbers of Jews. It may provide the rabbi with the challenge to write and speak extensively; in short, allowing a greater platform for his or her ideas. Because most organizations have the resources, the rabbi may also undertake research projects and depth studies on the many significant problems relating to the survival of Jewish life. Although most rabbis will not give up the satisfactions of the congregational rabbinate, some will see in the executive directorship new opportunities to be of service to their people and will feel challenged to undertake them.

The Rabbi as Educator

Recognizing the centrality of Jewish education to the perpetuation of the American Jewish community, communal and religious leaders have intensified their efforts in recent years to educate Jews—young and old alike. Synagogues, Hillels, day schools, camps, federations, and many other organizations have determined to provide the very highest level of Jewish instruction. Consequently, the Jewish educator has emerged as a new and vital professional role.

Jewish education is actually a career in itself. Today, it is possible to obtain a graduate degree in Jewish education from the Hebrew Union College–Jewish Institute of Religion, the

Jewish Theological Seminary, Yeshiva University, and other institutions of higher Jewish education. Jewish educators possessing pedagogic skills, administrative experience, and scholarship are in wide demand, and many rabbis (already themselves learned teachers) have made the field of Jewish education their specialty.

Considering the fact that Jewish education is universally recognized as crucial to the development of modern Jewish identity, it is no surprise that more and more positions have opened up over the past two decades. Perhaps the most startling educational growth may be seen in the Jewish day school. Recently, the Jewish Education Service of North America published a census of Jewish day-school students in North America. In the academic year 1982–1983, there were 587 day schools with an enrollment of 105,000 students. Moreover, the growth of the day-school movement may be seen in every movement in American Judaism: 75 percent of these schools were Orthodox in affiliation, 18 percent Conservative, 2 percent Reform, and 5 percent interdenominational. These institutions depend on Jewish educators to administer and supervise their programs.

As in many other specialized rabbinic careers, "rabbinic" educators/administrators often seek advanced degrees to equip themselves with the requisite skills. Some rabbis go on to earn master's and doctoral degrees in Jewish education. Ronald Kronish, a rabbi and educator, has stressed the importance of "rabbi-educators" in his article "The Rabbi as Educator":

> Rabbis ought to be more active in community-sponsored education, as members of the staffs of bureaus, as directors of community schools, and as teachers and curriculum developers in these schools. This will help restore our educational and spiritual links to k'lal yisrael, and it will benefit our synagogues and the community as a whole in a mutual exchange of talent, substance, and creativity.

Ancillary Professional Training for the Rabbi

For the rabbi to function effectively, it is essential to acquire skills that may not have been taught in depth in the highly specialized seminary program. Among these are pastoral counseling, social work, and community relations. The congregational rabbi often is called upon to function in such areas and should be proficient in them.

Some of the seminaries offer introductory courses in human relations, in which basic information of normal and abnormal psychology is imparted. The rabbinic student is made aware of the ebb and flow in the human life cycle. Becoming conscious of one's own limitations and problems enables one to avoid projecting them upon those who seek counsel. Such courses deal with the principles of group dynamics and social action. The role of the rabbi is critically examined, as is the structure and value system of the contemporary synagogue. Community problems are investigated, and the functions of social agencies are analyzed.

The rabbinic candidate is somewhat prepared to face the counseling or pastoral role, but he or she is far from expert in it. In all these relationships and roles, neither rabbinic student nor ordained rabbi must ever lose sight of the fact that Jews are seeking guidance from a rabbi qua rabbi. One's counsel should bear the impress of Jewish values while adhering to accepted guidance procedures. Rabbi Robert L. Katz, a pioneer and specialist in the field of human relations, has observed that because modern rabbis "will engage in more face-to-face counseling of individuals," they will "cease to rely exclusively in intuitive methods of counseling and will avail themselves of some of the insights, techniques, and cautions that have already been defined in the field of pastoral psychology." This means that the rabbi's education in this area of rabbinic work must be ongoing.

The normal areas of rabbinic counseling deal with the problems of marriage, divorce, educational and vocational difficulties and adjustments, illness, bereavement, and crises of various other kinds. The rabbi constantly deals with the question of religious faith or the loss thereof, as well as with the person on the verge of conversion into or out of the Jewish faith. A host of other problems are brought to the rabbi—some not worthy of the rabbi's time, others so complex that the rabbi should not become involved at all. The story is told of the Jewish matron who insisted upon seeing her rabbi because she suffered from a terrible headache. After telling her story in a torrent of words and screams, she finally paused to catch her breath and observed that her headache was gone. The rabbi moanfully replied that he was glad she had lost her headache, but as far as he was concerned, she had merely transferred it to *him*!

Even the rabbi who does not consider pastoral counseling his or her forte is obliged to become acquainted with the rudiments of therapy, if only to avoid making mistakes that may adversely affect the lives of others. Because the role of the clergy is growing and the rabbi's authority as a spokesperson for religion in the lives of families is recognized, the rabbi will be sought out with increasing frequency to counsel. A good heart and thoughtfulness are vital to successful counseling, but other traits must be acquired if the rabbi is to be effective. Rabbi Katz wisely admonishes, "When the rabbinical counselor listens, one should not take pride in the open but untrained ear." An overzealous counselor can do as much harm as no counselor at all. One must know where to draw the line. When the rabbi is presented with complex problems involving a great deal of time, it would be prudent to refer the people to the agencies having the appropriate professional personnel. If the rabbi is wise, he or she will make a study of all the available community resources to which one might direct people when possible and desirable.

In the early days of the American rabbinate, when congregations had special committees whose responsibility it was to take care of the indigent, people in search of work, and people in trouble, the synagogue served as a treatment center, however temporary such treatment may have been. A number of congregations, particularly the Free Synagogue in New

York, created a special Department of Social Service, which handled child adoption and care for the aged and the troubled. Today the picture is quite different. Ordinarily, rabbis are in close contact with the social service agencies and their staffs and work with them on such matters. There is hardly a community in America with a sizeable concentration of Jews that does not have a Jewish Family Service. Very often the rabbi is the key person, either as negotiator or as sponsor, from whom a reference is sought. The rabbi's reputation for keeping confidences must be impeccable, and his or her usefulness as a lay social worker is often measured by the extent to which a client can be helped quietly and efficiently. If the rabbi has a charitable fund, he or she will undoubtedly make proper use of it to help people in crisis situations. If such funds are lacking, there is always the Hebrew Free Loan Society to which the rabbi can turn, as well as generous members of the congregation.

Rabbi Sidney Goldstein (1879–1955), who for many years thrust the activities of the Free Synagogue into the social arena, wisely taught:

> The social ideas born of the souls of the Prophets can be realized only as they are painfully and courageously worked into the fabric of our social life. This the rabbi cannot accomplish alone. The rabbi must labor with and through men and women and groups and institutions. While the rabbi is not a professional social worker he [or she] is interested in the objectives of social work and must seek to participate in it on one's own level of competency, experience, and interest.

As teacher of the young, the rabbi is involved in youth work and camping. This area is developing as a distinct profession for a number of rabbis. There are some who are instinctively capable of relating to youth. Others have grown up in the various youth movements and show aptitude and preference for this type of work. They prepare themselves to become the professional heads of the youth and camping divisions of their respective movements. The national religious groupings have extensive programs for youth that supplement the formal study of the religious school. Often the camp and the youth programs are seen as extensions of the religious school. Supplementary curricula are prepared to make maximum use of these activities, which may take place outside the confines of the synagogue structure.

Every rabbi, however, becomes involved in such programs at one time or another, and it is important to be prepared when opportunities arise. A particular sensitivity is required to be successful in this work, and the rabbi needs to know in detail the problems that confront youth. When I was involved in a leadership training seminar in one of the Reform movement camps for "Living Judaism" several years ago, the subject scheduled to be taught was "The Hebrew Prophets." It became very clear, however, from the first moment of encounter with the young people who were nearing draft age, that their immediate concern was the issue of war and peace: their personal involvement in the military and the reconciliation of that involvement with the values that Judaism teaches. It took a skillful staff of rabbis to adapt the prepared materials to the particular needs of that encampment.

The rabbi is a communal leader. While he or she cannot participate actively in all causes simultaneously (for one could spend the entire day attending worthwhile meetings), the rabbi must nevertheless choose to become intensively involved in some. The congregation is part of a larger community, and both rabbi and congregants need to involve themselves in the welfare of that community. It is unwise for the rabbi to assume roles other than those of spiritual leader, spokesman, and teacher. In matters of community interest, the rabbi must be careful to attack issues and not personalities, to stand above the political manipulations that inevitably trouble every organization and stick to the religious and moral issues involved. The rabbi should strive to stand above the crowd and be a battler for principles rather than petty interests.

A new word has found a place recently in the religious vocabulary of Americans: *ecumenicity*. The term, which had a more limited meaning prior to the far-reaching conclusions of Vatican Council II, connoted a sort of worldwide reciprocity of recognition among Christian denominations. It has now been widened to include non-Christian religions as well. Ecumenicity goes beyond tolerating other religions to seeing inherent worth in them. Although there had been considerable interfaith activity before Vatican II, the 1965 declaration on the relation of the Roman Catholic Church to non-Christian religions opened the Church to searching dialogue with other religions. A large body of the world's populace that is Catholic has been able officially to relate to Jews as well as to other Christian communions because the Council's declaration largely swept away ancient grievances and hates that had no place in the modern world. During the two decades since the promulgation of Vatican II, a massive breakdown in stereotyped thinking has been taking place as Christians and Jews face one another to discuss their common traditions and destinies.

The condemnation of anti-Semitism by the First Assembly of the World Council of Churches (Protestant) in 1948 and the Vatican II pronouncement that "decries hatred, persecutions, displays of anti-Semitism" made possible new ways of interfaith programming. Increasingly, the rabbi is being called upon to engage in interfaith dialogue and seminars. It has been customary for some time and in some communities for rabbis and ministers to exchange pulpits to explain their respective faiths. Programming in depth, however, is now under way so that a full meeting can take place between Christians and Jews. The rabbi's training and attitudes require preparation for this important clerical activity, and a rabbi must be prepared to discuss the beliefs and principles of Judaism on the most profound and scholarly levels with religious leaders of comparable training and experience in the Christian ministry.

So much depends on attitude in interfaith work. Past rebuffs and animosities must be forgotten and new attempts made to reach understanding and appreciation for what has been called the Judeo-Christian heritage. The rabbi must also train fellow Jews and prepare them for an ecumenicity that will provide equal representation for Jewish laity in the religious affairs of the modern world. Joint commissions of Jews and Christians on civil rights, war and peace, poverty, and education have come into being. The rabbi's knowledge must encompass a historical understanding of the development of Christianity and its many denominations. In any event, this newest phase of rabbinic activity will continue to propel the rabbi into still other facets of interreligious community life.

The Jewish people want and expect the teachers of their faith to be involved in vital areas of community activity and demand their participation in decisions that affect the community. Not a charitable campaign is waged, not a community decision is made, in which some rabbis are not consulted. I recall that a Federation Council of a large city, which had made it a practice to avoid nominating rabbis for its board, received a rude awakening when a public write-in vote elected three rabbis to that board. Every rabbi, of course, has his or her own predilections and causes that assume more than nominal interest, where the rabbi is more than a statistic on a membership list.

Certainly, a part of every rabbi's commitment is to the rabbinical organization of both the movement and the community. The Board of Rabbis of a community, whether it consists of three or thirty members, represents the single voice of the Jewish clergy of that city. A wise rabbi cultivates meaningful friendships with colleagues. When rabbis stand together on matters of vital concern to the spiritual health and welfare of their community, they represent a force with which the community must reckon. Individually and collectively, the rabbis should be the religious and moral backbone of their community. If they succeed in this endeavor, their authority will be far-reaching and their effect will be felt.

Finding Your Own Level
Rabbi Jacob Weinstein (1902–1974) concluded:

The fact is that there are more than enough shared issues and great purposes to challenge any rabbi's heart and energies. Whether they will lead to a great rabbinic career is not the important question. The question is, will it help to move humankind a little closer to the good society? A rabbi who demands greatness from this profession, in the sense of prominence and prestige, is really in the wrong calling. A rabbi who sees no greatness even in the humble tasks of ministering to a congregation, in sermons, pastoral calls, ceremonial and honorific chores, will not achieve greatness in the larger arena. A rabbi who does not get supreme satisfaction from having helped others on the road to greatness will never achieve it . . . The horizon is full of great issues. They are larger than the human fist so that any Elijah can read even while running. A rabbi who does not see the bush burning, nor feel the fire, nor hear the call in every vagrant mind, cannot be sincere. Such ears are waxed. Such eyes are blinded from looking outside for the glory which should be found within.

In those telling words, Rabbi Weinstein enjoined every colleague to find his or her own level, realize his or her own capacities, and then work to develop them to the utmost. It is wise for the rabbi to take stock of professional assets and liabilities. It is important for the young rabbi, in particular, to work diligently to strengthen whatever gifts he or she may have and to bring into prominence the unusual capacities that give some contour and structure to the rabbinate.

An important question in conjunction with finding one's own level is where the rabbi wishes to become established. Sometimes personal considerations determine in what part of the country the rabbi will settle. One may be drawn to the prospect of a large or a small congregation. As might be expected, the greatest number of rabbis is found in large cities, where big congregations abound. Yet many prefer to serve congregations in smaller communities. In these situations, the rabbi might very well be the only Jewish clergyman in town. Under no other set of circumstances is the rabbi needed as much. The rabbi in a small community is often the exemplar of the Jewish faith to the non-Jewish community. The rabbi's advice and assistance are sought on all types of communal projects, Jewish and secular. The rabbi's life may be less hectic than that of colleagues in the larger centers of populations, yet the rabbi in a small community usually knows congregants and participants more intimately in their lives.

Many accomplished rabbis who now serve large metropolitan synagogues started in smaller towns. The years of preparation and training that such opportunities afford are invaluable in their benefit to vocational growth and success. In other instances, rabbis gravitate directly toward large clusters of Jewish population. These areas yield extensive opportunities for service and involvement in an active Jewish community with established schools and communal institutions.

The rabbinate in the big city provides much variation. One may choose to be the spiritual leader of a small, or smaller, congregation in the suburbs, or in time, with seniority and seasoning, of a large metropolitan congregation. There are certain rigors that the rabbi in the big town must undergo. One may drive as much as a hundred miles in fulfilling a day's responsibilities, to hospital calls, cemeteries, weddings, and meetings. The necessity of budgeting time becomes very important under such circumstances. Yet no matter how well the rabbi accomplishes this task, some frustration is inevitable, simply because there are only seven days in a week and some sixteen or eighteen waking hours in a day. It is therefore important for the rabbi to learn discipline and to establish priorities within a work schedule. Much like an old-time movie serial, no matter how much the rabbi does, the ending is always "to be continued."

Rabbi Richard C. Hertz, rabbi emeritus of a large congregation, once raised the questions:

> What distinguishes a rabbi in a large congregation from one serving in a small community? Is it by the number of weddings at which the rabbi officiates? Is it by the number

of hospital calls and sick calls and condolence calls made? Is it by the number of consultations in the rabbi's study on marital problems, family problems, teenage problems, personal problems, community problems, organizational problems?

It is clear that volume and accelerated pace characterize the rabbinate of a large congregation in a metropolis. The pastoral rabbinate of the big city is no different in substance from that of the small suburban city. Rabbi Hertz, in discussing this point, observed:

> People are people ... The rabbi's life is with people. During the course of the day, the rabbi may preach and teach, pray and play, laugh and cry, go from a funeral to a wedding reception to a hospital room ... While some deal in steel, some in stone, some in dollars, some in goods, a rabbi deals with human hearts ... A congregation is, after all, people. Not a building, not an edifice, not a new temple nor an old temple, but people of all ages, of all interests and lack of interest.

The rabbinate must be qualitative, whatever the activities and their number. The temptation to view as just so many statistics the weddings, funerals, b'nai mitzvah, and other ritual-centered duties of the rabbi is ever-present. Because of the pressure of work, it is a constant challenge to view each event as of importance. For example, the rabbi may be performing his or her thousandth wedding, but the ceremony for this couple must not be routine or impersonal; for *that* couple it is their *first* wedding. All the warmth and spontaneity the rabbi can summon is needed to make the ceremony meaningful. The same condition holds true for the other rabbinic duties and rites. One's teaching and administrative capacity, as well as one's ability to make vital the ritual aspects of Jewish life, represent the indices of the rabbi's effectiveness. The rabbi needs to take people's problems seriously, but himself or herself not too seriously.

As Rabbi Hertz noted, a rabbi can wear any kind of shirt or blouse—button-down, tab, blue, white, or dress shirt—but one should never wear "a stuffed shirt." That's good advice, important to remember even in the most prestigious moments of a rabbi's career.

Finding one's own level in the rabbinate is the result of conscious resolve, trial and error, and circumstance. For instance, there have been rabbis who accepted a call to a certain position only as a temporary post and twenty years later were still in the same pulpit. This was not because of inertia but because they chose to respond to growing challenges that were not initially anticipated. The fabled Rabbi Henry Cohen (1863–1952) was known as "the man who stayed in Texas." This pioneer rabbi chose the difficult task of bringing Judaism to a frontier of American life. He "stayed" in Galveston for 63 years to finish his work! Other rabbis move from congregation to congregation until they find a compatible one. Whether in the smaller community or in the larger city, the rabbi should strive to develop his or her own strong interests. These may be the synagogue exclusively, serious scholarship, civic life, or some combination of these activities. The rabbi finds fulfillment in work as long as he or she remains productive. The rabbi's own reservoir of talent, enthusiasm, and dedication needs to be constantly replenished so that work remains stimulating and challenging.

It is for energizing interest in Jewish life and existence that the rabbi was ordained. The path is not an easy one; it is filled with thorns as well as roses, stumbling blocks as well as milestones. Inclement weather of discouragement may threaten the benevolent sunshine of friendship and promise. Yet for a good number of Jewish idealists it is the only road they choose to walk, for they have that deep and abiding feeling within them, "For this I was created."

Chapter V

The Rabbi and the Future of the American Jew

Twenty years ago, when I first set down my views on this topic, I wrote these words:

Throughout recent years we have read debates on whether or not the American Jew was "vanishing." It is concluded in the discussions that we will vanish only if we lose our Jewish consciousness which, while difficult to define, is readily recognizable when it is encountered. This consciousness involves the conviction that one is part of a great people which has had an illustrious yet trying history. Within that history there are marked eras in which Judaism was on the decline, and others in which it was in great efflorescence.

The future of the American Jewish community still pivots, I believe, on the presence of that "Jewish consciousness." Yet, the past two decades have driven home the realization that our contemporary existence in America has no true historical precedent. As noted, Jewish history is characterized by a succession of eras, some boasting tremendous advances and others plagued by oppression and difficulty. The imminent dawn of the twenty-first century brings with it the comprehension of the stunning paradox of Jewish life in America: *We are at once the most advantaged and the most disadvantaged Jewry in the long history of our people*. Dr. Jacob Rader Marcus, the dean of American Jewish historians, has eloquently described the hospitable atmosphere in which the American Jew currently thrives:

> In no instance has the Jew encountered the situation, similar to that in this great land, where every hope and yearning is in full consonance with those of his neighbors, where the ideals for which the Jew has in the past sacrificed life and possessions form the very cornerstone of its structure, and where participation in the common weal is assured as of right rather than by sufferance.

The undeniable truth of Dr. Marcus' characterization must be tempered by a recognition of the formidable problems that threaten to erode the very foundation of our communal structure.

Some observers have argued that Jewish illiteracy in America poses the gravest threat to the community's infrastructure. Indeed, American Jewry may be the most affluent, the most politically adept in history. But most agree that we are simultaneously the most ignorant Jewry—speaking in terms of Jewish knowledge. In his illuminating study on "Jewish Education in the United States," Professor Lloyd P. Gartner stressed that very point:

> Jewish education was better established and financed during the 1950's and 1960's than ever before. At the same time, the level of Jewish knowledge among American Jews lagged further and further beneath their general educational attainment as study, that ancient cynosure, inspired young Jews in almost every field except that in which it originated. *By the standard of centuries, American Jews are functionally illiterate as Jews.*

American Jews are not merely ignorant Jews, they are often nonparticipatory Jews. In the context of our open, free society, no Jew is compelled to participate in the Jewish community. Some estimate that as many as 60 percent of

America's Jews do not associate with any organized Jewish activity. Moreover, Jewish religious observance, in the home as well as in the synagogue, has waned. In his book *The Mask Jews Wear*, Professor Eugene Borowitz of the Hebrew Union College–Jewish Institute of Religion has dubbed our generation of Jews "inverted Marranos." The Marranos of fifteenth- and sixteenth-century Spain and Portugal lived outwardly as Christians while inwardly, in the privacy of their own homes, they struggled to preserve their Jewish religious identity. American Jews proclaim themselves to be Jews outwardly, while in *their* homes and in *their* synagogues they frequently practice nothing at all. Commenting on this phenomenon, Rabbi Abraham Joshua Heschel wrote:

> One stands aghast before the multitudes of our people . . .
> A generation of Jews has arisen that knows not the Torah, that knows not how to distinguish between the Sabbath and the weekdays, between the sacred and the sensational.

American rabbis in the twenty-first century will have the historic task of confronting these challenges. Actually, the future vitality of Jewish life in America will turn on the quality of rabbinic leadership and the innovations that tomorrow's rabbis will bring to bear on these communal concerns. The prophets of doom say that the problems are too onerous and the hour is already late. Yet I agree with the teaching of our talmudic sage Rabbi Tarfon, who proclaimed *Lo alecha ha-melachah lig-mor* . . .

> You may not finish the task, but neither are you free to desist from it. The day is short, and the task is great, but the "Commanding Voice" urges you forward . . . (Avot II, 20–21)

It is the rabbi's primary obligation to perpetuate the Jewish consciousness and to deepen it in successive generations of Jews by personal example and teaching. These pressing issues —Jewish literacy and communal participation—are central to the maintenance of that Jewish consciousness. All the rabbi's skills, learned through years of hard experience, as well as the vast fund of knowledge, secular and sacred, that has been garnered, must be devoted to this task.

In addition is the recognition that the great lessons of the Jewish past must be brought to bear upon our contemporary world. The greatest religious precept that Judaism has bequeathed to humanity is that of ethical monotheism: the Oneness of God and its derivative principle, the unity of humanity. Jews have taught the need for social justice in the world and have been involved in the critical upheavals that have led to the advance of human civilization. In the coming century, the rabbinate will be increasingly faced with the task of assimilating the insights and methods of western civilization and harmonizing them with the historic truths of Judaism. Tomorrow's rabbis, inheritors of the prophetic tradition, will have to remain zealous to see that the computer age does not lead to computerized feelings, computerized allegiance, computerized love—in short, the snuffing out of the human element in our earthly existence. By training and by predilection, the rabbi is that singular individual in Jewish society who is able and ready to address the emerging needs of American Jewry and American culture.

Most recently, the topic of Jewish unity (or, phrased negatively, Jewish disunity) has become a central issue on the agenda of many American Jews. Dr. Irving Greenberg, President of the National Jewish Center for Learning and Leadership, is recognized as the first Jewish spokesperson to acknowledge the centrality of this topic to the perpetuation of Jewish consciousness. Dr. Greenberg's essay, "Will There Be One Jewish People by the Year 2000?", forewarns that the "current cycle of alienation, hostility, and withdrawal ... [may very well] lead to a sundering of the Jewish people into two religions or two social groups, fundamentally divided and opposed to each other."

As the acknowledged leaders and authoritative interpreters of Jewish tradition, rabbis will undoubtedly play a crucial role in the outcome of this debate on Jewish unity. The possible fracturing of our fragile communal bond—and a tenuous link it is that connects the broad spectrum of Jewish life—can be averted only if rabbinic leadership of all movements is determined to invoke the principles of unity, not uniformity, a common heritage over current areas of divergence. It is safe to assert that the quality and stature of our community's rabbis will affect the ultimate resolution of this question.

The future of the American Jew is indissolubly connected with the future of Israel. While Israel is a political state, it is also the spiritual and cultural center of world Jewry. Because of the decimation of the religious and secular institutions of Russian Jewry, only American Jewry stands on an equal footing with the Jew in Israel in the capacity to create a meaningful Jewish life. Israeli life and letters already have made a great impression on American Jewry. Hebrew has been reborn as a living tongue. As Israelis are making an attempt to understand Diaspora Jewry, so American Jewry must come to grips with developments in Israel. Intellectual currents are never contained by geographic borders. With the interchange of students between the two countries, of professors and of ideologies, Israelis will move into ever closer orbit to the thinking of the American Jew and vice versa. Living bridges of people, traveling freely between these two centers of Jewish civilization, will create a strong bond between us.

I believe that Israeli Jewry can learn much from American Jewry, particularly in regard to the freedom of its religious life. Both philosophically and structurally, religious Judaism has become a force in America because the bedrock of its development was freedom of conscience. The American rabbi of the Conservative and Reform traditions has few counterparts in Israel. Non-Orthodox Judaism in Israel is in its fledgling state, but it will grow because it is within the nature of Judaism itself to promote democratic institutions rather than oligarchies.

The rabbi also has an obligation to world Jewry. A rabbi who loves the Jewish people will embrace the Yemenite, the

Indian, the North African Jew as members of the family; a rabbi must be concerned for their fate and the future of their existence. This concern inevitably propels the American rabbi into activities that will make it possible for Jews in all parts of the world to perpetuate themselves. Generalizing from the American experience, the rabbi will come to the conclusion that democratic institutions need assistance and support throughout the world. Jews are the barometers of history. In lands of persecution where restraint still exists on the freedom of thought and belief, Jews and Judaism suffer first. Wherever divisiveness and hatred flourish, the vise of antagonistic parties oppresses the Jew. It is in the interest of the American rabbi, both as a matter of principle and hard reality, to promote the idea of a world community to assure basic human rights. Such, after all, was the vision of the Hebrew prophet who dreamed of a world free of war, a world in which all humankind could dwell together with "none to make them afraid."

As interfaith, interracial, and intercultural activities abound in the "ecumenical age," the universal teachings of Judaism will possess particular relevance. The rabbi must, in fact, be devoted not only to teaching the mandates of Judaism to his or her people, but through them and others to the widest periphery in our world. Judaism has always been a religion that underscored its mission to teach the Torah to the world. The rabbi, as teacher of that tradition, has both opportunity and responsibility to expand and continue the system of truths evolved by the Jewish people in its encounter with God and the world. Trained to serve the Jewish people, the rabbi can bring these teachings to fruition. Rabbi Abba Hillel Silver taught, "The mission ideal . . . is of the very warp and woof of prophetic Judaism. It is valid today. It is the burden of our destiny . . ." This, in substance, remains the mandate of the modern American rabbi. The task is a hard, challenging, historic one. Perhaps *you* are one who should respond to it.

Appendix **A**

THE AMERICAN RABBINATE, 1960-1986: A BIBLIOGRAPHIC ESSAY by GARY P. ZOLA

Students wishing to explore the American rabbinate more thoroughly will find no shortage of articles, essays, monographs, and books devoted to the topic. This essay attempts to organize this vast material into a more manageable format. What follows does not presume to be an exhaustive bibliography, but rather a description and evaluation of those works that contribute most significantly to an understanding of the *contemporary* American rabbinate. As such, reference to works written by or about rabbis prior to 1960 have generally been excluded. Readers may also refer to bibliographies in Norman Linzer, ed., *Jewish Communal Services in the United States: 1960–1970* (New York: Commision on Synagogue Relations, 1972), pp. 128–248; and Elliot L. Stevens, ed., *Rabbinic Authority: Papers Presented Before the Ninety-First Annual Convention of the Central Conference of American Rabbis* (New York: CCAR, 1982), pp. 111–118. The *Encyclopaedia Judaica* (Jerusalem. Keter Publishing, 1972) essay on the rabbinate (vol. 13, pp. 1445–1458) includes a brief bibliography that highlights pre–1960 contributions.

HISTORY

The only full-scale history analyzing the American rabbinate is Jacob Rader Marcus and Abraham J. Peck, eds., *The American Rabbinate*: *Century of Continuity and Change, 1883-1983* (Hoboken: Ktav Publishing House, New Jersey, 1985). This book is not an integrated analysis, but consists of three essays on the Orthodox, Conservative, and Reform rabbinates respectively. (Students interested in the earliest stages of rabbinic leadership in the United States should see Jacob Rader Marcus, *The Handsome Young Priest in the Black Gown*: *The Personal World of Gershom Seixas* [Cincinnati: American Jewish Archives, 1970], and Bertram W. Korn, "Isaac Leeser: Centennial Reflections," *American Jewish Archives* 19 [1967]: pp. 127-141; Maxwell Whiteman, "Isaac Leeser and the Jews of Philadelphia," *Publication of the American Jewish Historical Society* 48 [1959]: pp. 207-244; and also Lance J. Sussman's fine Ph.D. dissertation on Leeser. See also Jonathan D. Sarna, "The Spectrum of Jewish Leadership in Ante-Bellum America," *Journal of American Ethnic History,* Spring (1982): pp. 59-67.) In "The Image of the Rabbis, Formerly and Today" (an essay in *Steeled by Adversity* [Philadelphia: Jewish Publication Society of America, 1971], pp. 147-157), Salo W. Baron offers a noteworthy comparison between the contemporary American rabbinate and its historical counterpart. Abraham J. Karp's biographical studies on pioneering Orthodox rabbis are vital to any student wishing to explore the history of American Orthodox Judaism: "New York Chooses a Chief Rabbi," XLIV *Publications of the American Jewish Historical Society* (1954): pp. 129ff; "Solomon Schechter Comes to America," LIII *American Jewish Historical Quarterly* (1963): pp. 44ff; and "The Ridwas, Rabbi Jacob David Wilowsky 1845-1913," in Arthur A. Chiel, ed., *Perspectives on Jews and Judaism*: *Essays in Honor of Wolfe Kelman* (New York: Rabbinical Assembly, 1978), pp. 215-238.

Sidney B. Hoenig traces the history of the Orthodox rabbinate in the military chaplaincy from the start of the French and Indian War through 1976 in "The Orthodox Rabbi as a Military Chaplain, A Bicentennial Retrospect," *Tradition* Fall (1976): pp. 35-60. (This article is enhanced by several helpful appendices, including a list of Orthodox chaplains on active duty from 1940 to 1976.) The history and structure of the Orthodox rabbinate in the United States is of central concern to Menachem Friedman, "The Changing Role of the Community Rabbinate," *Jerusalem Quarterly* 25 (1982): pp. 79–99. The impact of the congregational rabbinate (especially the Reform rabbinate) on the civil rights movement in the United States is thoughtfully portrayed in Allen P. Krause, "Rabbis and Negro Rights in the South, 1954–1967," *American Jewish Archives* XXI (1969): pp. 20–47.

Histories of the major seminaries in the United States constitute an additional resource for reconstructing the development of the American rabbi: Michael A. Meyer, "A Centennial History," *Hebrew Union College–Jewish Institute of Religion at One Hundred Years* (Cincinnati: Hebrew Union College Press, 1976); Chapter VI, "The Conservative Rabbi," in Marshall Sklare's *Conservative Judaism* (New York: Schocken Books, 1972), pp. 159–198; Moshe Davis, *The Emergence of Conservative Judaism* (Philadelphia: The Burning Bush Press, 1963); Herbert Parzen, *Architects of Conservative Judaism* (New York: J. David, 1964); Gilbert Klaperman, *The Story of Yeshiva University: The First Jewish University in America* (New York: Macmillan, 1969), and William B. Helmreich's *The World of the Yeshivah* (New York: Free Press, 1982), which is an illuminating sociological study on life in the American yeshivah. Two essays that shed light on salient issues in the world of the American yeshivah today (and indirectly on the nature of the Orthodox rabbinate) are "Trends in the American Yeshivah Today," by Oscar Z. Fasman in *Tradition: A Journal of Orthodox Jewish Thought* 9 (Fall 1967): pp. 48–64; and "Trends in the American *Yeshivot*: A Rejoinder," by Emanuel Feldman in *Tradition: A Journal of Orthodox Jewish Thought* 9 (Spring 1968): pp. 56–64. (Both of these essays are reprinted in Reuven P. Bulka, ed., *Dimensions of Orthodox Judaism* [New York: Ktav Publishing House, 1983]: pp. 317–336.) Louis Bernstein's *Challenge and*

Mission: The Emergence of the English Speaking Orthodox Rabbinate (New York: Shengold Publishers, 1982) is primarily an organizational history of the Rabbinical Council of America. The most recent Supplement Volume (1983–5) of the *Encyclopaedia Judaica* devotes an entire section (pp. 84–105) to "The Making of American Rabbis." The curricula of the Reform, Reconstructionist, Conservative, and Orthodox seminaries are fully described in this chapter. Earlier studies include Charles S. Liebman's critical evaluation of the nature of rabbinic education in America, "The Training of American Rabbis," *American Jewish Yearbook* LXIX (1968): pp. 3–112, which sparked a series of counterevaluations including Avis Shulman's, "How American Rabbis are Trained," *Reconstructionist* XXXV (1969): pp. 7–13; Levi A. Olan, "The Rabbi in a Secular World," *Reconstructionist* XXXV (1969): pp. 13–15; and a fascinating symposium of colleagues who debated "The Future of Rabbinic Training in America," *Judaism* 18 (1969): pp. 387–420.

BIOGRAPHIES AND AUTOBIOGRAPHIES

Biographical and autobiographical works unquestionably constitute a vital resource for the study of the American rabbinate. Literally hundreds of books, essays, and articles have been written to memorialize the life and work of American rabbis. Again, it is not within the scope of this essay to itemize the extant material on rabbis who lived and worked in the United States prior to 1960. Instead we confine our attention to biographies and autobiographies dealing with contemporary rabbis (since 1960) whose life and work shed light on the nature of the rabbinate today.

The Orthodox congregational rabbinate is well portrayed in Immanuel Jakobovitz's autobiographical *Journal of a Rabbi* (New York: Living Books, 1966). Aaron I. Reichel's biography of his grandfather, *The Maverick Rabbi: Rabbi Herbert S. Goldstein and the Institutional Synagogue—"A New Organizational Form"* (Norfolk, Virginia: Donning,

1984) is a highly filiopietistic, albeit interesting account of an innovative Orthodox leader. Samuel Rosenblatt's autobiography *The Days of My Years* (New York: Ktav Publishing House, 1976) offers yet another perspective on the congregational rabbinate in the Orthodox community. A realistic and informative look at the contemporary Conservative rabbinate is provided by Stuart E. Rosenberg, *The Real Jewish World: A Rabbi's Second Thoughts* (New York: Philosophical Library, 1984). Constantly vacillating between biography and autobiography, Israel Mowshowitz's *A Rabbi's Rovings* (Hoboken, New Jersey: Ktav Publishing House, 1985) illumines the active and varied career of this Conservative rabbi. Janice J. Feldstein's *Rabbi Jacob J. Weinstein: Advocate of the People* (New York: Ktav Publishing House, 1980) is a competent biography detailing the life of a Reform leader in Chicago. Weinstein's involvement with social action causes may be compared to the less well-written but nevertheless important biography of the social activist Reform rabbi of Atlanta, *One Voice: Rabbi Jacob M. Rothschild and the Troubled South* (Macon, GA: Mercer University Press, 1985), written by his widow, Janice Rothschild Blumberg. The role of the rabbi in the South is further explored in several essays in *Turn to the South* edited by Nathan M. Kaganoff and Melvin J. Urofsky (Charlottesville, Virginia: University Press of Virginia, 1979). These include "Portrait of a Romantic Rebel: Bernard C. Ehrenreich (1876–1955)" by Byron L. Sherwin, "The Role of the Rabbi in the South" by Malcolm H. Stern, "The Rabbi in Miami—A Case History" by Gladys Rosen, and Jack D. Spiro's "Rabbi in the South: A Personal View." Mark K. Bauman's and Arnold Shankman's illuminating essay, "The Rabbi as Ethnic Broker: The Case of David Marx," *American Ethnic History* 2 (Spring 1983): pp. 51–68, is a useful analysis of the role the Reform rabbi played in the South during the first half of the twentieth century.

Roland B. Gittelsohn's personal reflections "On Being a Rabbi: Then and Now," *Journal of Reform Judaism*, Spring (1981): pp. 77–78, offer a captivating analysis of how the

Reform rabbinate evolved between 1936 and 1980. The nature of the Reform rabbinate in Montreal, Canada (a city in which Reform Judaism constitutes a minority of the Jewish population), is portrayed in the autobiographical *Harry Joshua Stern* (New York: Bloch Publishing Co., 1981). William G. Braude's autobiographical essay, "Recollections of a Septuagenarian," *Rhode Island Jewish Historical Notes* 8 (November 1981): pp. 345–372 and (November 1982): pp. 401–441, is an intriguing look at the evolution of this scholarly Reform rabbi during his more than fifty years in the American rabbinate. Recent autobiographies of prominent Reform rabbis also include W. Gunther Plaut's *Unfinished Business* (Toronto: Lester and Orpen Dennys, 1981) and Julian B. Feibelman's *The Making of a Rabbi* (New York: Vantage Press, 1980).

There also exist several personal accounts of rabbinic work outside the congregational sphere. One Orthodox rabbi's dedication to a *Landsmanshaft* (Jewish fraternal organization) is traced in Sol Landau, *Bridging Two Worlds*: *Rabbi Ezekiel Landau (1888–1965)* (New York: J. David, 1968). Landau, a refugee from Nazi persecution, established upon his arrival in this country the Jewish Friends Society, a mutual-aid organization for new immigrants. Although he was primarily a congregational rabbi, Solomon Goldman attained a national reputation as a result of his numerous outside organizational activities. Jacob J. Weinstein's biography *Solomon Goldman*: *A Rabbi's Rabbi* (New York: Ktav Publishing House, 1973) is an excellent reconstruction of this towering leader's rabbinate. Similarly, Israel Goldstein's *My World as a Jew* (New York: Herzl Press, 1984) is an example of autobiographical writing at its best. Like Goldman, Conservative Rabbi Israel Goldstein's impact on the American rabbinate, Zionism, politics, and the State of Israel reflects the rich diversity of contemporary rabbinic activity in the United States. The Reform movement has its share of institutional giants too; Sam Cauman's *Jonah Bondi Wise* (New York: Crown Publishers, 1966) is a critically written account of the life of Issac M. Wise's son, who was himself an enormously influential rabbinic leader. Marc Lee Raphael's forthcoming biography of Abba Hillel Silver will provide a long awaited full-scale account of this towering figure. Stephen S. Wise died before 1960 (1949), but his imposing career parallels those of Goldman, Goldstein, Wise, and Silver in many important ways. Melvin I. Urofsky has produced a fine biography, *A Voice That Spoke for Justice: The Life and Times of Stephen S. Wise* (Albany, New York: Suny Press, 1982). *Stephen S. Wise, Servant of the People* (Philadelphia: Jewish Publication Society of America, 1969), edited by Carl Hermann Voss, is a compilation of Wise's most significant letters and speeches. Unfortunately, the only published biography of famed Biblical Archaeologist and HUC–JIR president, Nelson Glueck, is Ellen N. Stern's narrowly conceived *Dreamer in the Desert: A Profile of Nelson Glueck* (New York: Ktav Publishing House, 1980).

The roles of the rabbi in the B'nai B'rith Hillel Foundations is well portrayed through the writings of Albert S. Axelrad, *Meditations of a Maverick Rabbi* (Chappaqua, New York: Rossel Books, 1984). Hersh Livazer's autobiography *The Rabbi's Blessing: From the Memories of a Chaplain in the U.S. Army, 1943–1965* (Jerusalem: H. Livazer, 1980) provides an interesting account (if one can overlook the numerous editing errors) of the military chaplaincy from an Orthodox perspective. Conservative Rabbi Hillel E. Silverman recounts his experiences in the military chaplain's corps, "A Congregation that Salutes Its Rabbi," *Jewish Digest*, XII (1967): pp. 75–78. The work of the rabbi as hospital chaplain is sensitively described in Joseph Levine, "Bikur Holim: A Clinical Perspective," *Journal of Reform Judaism* (Summer, 1979): pp. 25–34. In "Counseling of the Well-Aged: A Guide for Rabbis," *Journal of Reform Judaism* (Summer, 1981): pp. 35–40, Albert M. Lewis describes the nature of rabbinic care for the elderly.

SOCIOLOGICAL STUDIES

Murray Polner, *Rabbi: The American Experience* (New York: Holt, Rinehart and Winston, 1977) and Gilbert Rosenthal, ed., *The American Rabbi* (New York: Ktav Publishing House, 1977) are excellent overviews of the modern rabbinate in the United States. Polner concentrated on the congregational experience whereas Rosenthal assembled articles stressing the rich diversity in contemporary rabbinic endeavor (chaplaincy, Hillels, scholarship, education, organization, and so forth).

The report of Theodore Lenn and Associates, *Rabbi and Synagogue in Reform Judaism* (Commission by the CCAR; New York, 1972) remains the most controversial sociological study on the American Reform rabbinate. Much ink has been spilled in response to Lenn's largely unflattering evaluation of the state of the Reform rabbinate. (Cf. Julius Weinberg, "The Trouble with Reform Judaism," *Commentary* [November, 1979]: pp. 53–60, who defends Lenn's conclusion; and Jacob Neusner, "Is the Conservative Movement Losing Strength?", *Boston Jewish Advocate* [20 December 1984], who offers an opposing perspective. See also Eugene B. Borowitz's response to Lenn in "R**e**nconstructing the Rabbinate: An Open Letter to Dr. Theodore I. Lenn," *CCAR Journal* XVII [1970]: pp. 59–64, as well as an entire issue of the *CCAR Journal* devoted to "Afterthoughts on Lenn," [Winter 1973]).

Lenn's conclusions about the Reform rabbinate came on the heels of a spate of essays bemoaning what was conceived to be a general malaise in the American rabbinate. Morris Adler, "The Rabbi: 1966," *Jewish Heritage* 8 (1966): pp. 7–9, contended that the American rabbi reflected the "frustrations, ambivalences, confusions and uncertainties which pervaded the Jewish community in general." The contemporary function and importance of a rabbi in America was seriously questioned by Arthur Hertzberg, "The Changing American Rabbinate," *Midstream*, XII (1966): 16–29. Jacob J. Weinstein contradicted Hertzberg's conclusions in "Contra Hertzberg: On the Changing American Rabbinate," *CCAR Journal*, XIII (1966): pp. 70–74. A decade later, Hertzberg's pessimistic viewpoint appeared to have been tempered considerably in "The

Changing Rabbinate," *Proceedings of the Rabbinical Assembly* 37 (New York: 1975). (Cf. Charles Liebman's essay critically evaluating seminary curricula, mentioned supra.) Congregant ambivalence toward rabbis and problems of rabbinic image are the focus of Jordan I. Taxon, "The Image of the American Rabbi—God's Restless and Lonely Man," *Jewish Digest*, XI (1965): pp. 25-28.

In recent years, the Orthodox rabbinate has experienced a modest amount of sociological scrutiny as well. Ralph Pelcovitz's *Danger and Opportunity: Essays on Traditional Judaism in a Time of Crisis* (New York: Shengold Publishers, 1976) contains a fascinating chapter entitled "The Rabbi and the Rosh Yeshiva." In it, Pelcovitz laments the recent communal trend of diminishing the traditional role of the congregational Orthodox rabbi as legal decisor and learned teacher in favor of yeshivah academicians.

Much attention has been given to the matter of restructuring the role of the rabbi in response to contemporary realities. Abraham J. Feldman, "Dwelling Together in Harmony," *CCAR Journal* XIII (1965): pp. 45-50, suggests that congregational support for and interest in the rabbi's activities may ultimately defuse relationship problems that plague the two. Simon Greenberg points to the undefined nature of a rabbi's role as the source of professional discontent in "The Rabbinate and the Jewish Community," *Conservative Judaism* XXIII (1969): 52-67. Understanding the transformation of modern society informs the rabbi, wrote Abraham J. Karp, of the new demands that must be faced in "Rabbi, Congregation, and the World They Live In," *Conservative Judaism* XXVI (1971): pp. 25-40.

Robert L. Katz, a pioneer in the field of rabbinic interpersonal relations, wrote more than a dozen essays on the nature of rabbinic/congregational relations. Katz argued for a redefinition of accepted styles of rabbinic leadership in "The Future of the Rabbinate—Ascribed vs. Achieved Leadership, Perspectives from Sociology," *CCAR Journal*, XVII (1970): pp. 49-65. In "Changing Self-Concepts of Reform Rabbis 1976," *CCAR Journal* (Summer, 1976): pp.

51–56, Katz recommended that contemporary rabbis should become less distant, more human. Daniel Jeremy Silver's most recent article on the rabbinate, "The Core of Our Calling: Who Is a Rabbi? What Is a Rabbi? Why Is a Rabbi?", *Journal of Reform Judaism* (Spring, 1986): pp. 1–28 is a provocative essay analyzing the contemporary nature of rabbinic effectiveness. Silver's earlier essay, "The Worth of the Work We Do," *CCAR Journal*, XVII (1970): pp. 81–88, is a helpful analysis of both the frustrations and satisfactions inherent in the modern rabbinate. The importance of honing mediation skills for the modern rabbinate is stressed by Harold Schulweis, "Helping Rabbis Be Shul Wise," *Moment* (January/February 1984: pp. 38–41). The modern rabbi is part priest and part prophet, but Henry Bamberger argued that the priestly role is his favorite, "Confessions of an Unashamed Priest," *CCAR Journal*, XIX (1972): pp. 109–111. Another sociological perspective on the Reform rabbinate may be found throughout Norman Mirsky's book *Unorthodox Judaism* (Columbus, Ohio: Ohio State University Press, 1978), but see specifically chapters four and five entitled "Why Me, Lord?" and "A Rabbi Named Sally", respectively.

The sources of rabbinic authority in contemporary society have been analyzed most thoroughly in Elliot Stevens, ed., *Op. Cit.*, and in Jacob Neusner, ed., *Understanding American Judaism*, 2 vols. (New York: Ktav Publishing House, 1975). Volume One of the latter deals with the rabbi and the synagogue; contributing essays explore the education and character of the contemporary American rabbi as well as the source of today's rabbinic authority. The first significant (and still frequently noted) study on the sources of authority in the contemporary rabbinate is Jerome E. Carlin's and Saul H. Mendlovitz's "The American Rabbi: A Religious Specialist Responds to Loss of Authority," in Marshall Sklare, ed., *The Jews* (Glencoe, IL: Free Press, 1958), pp. 377–414. Daniel J. Elazar and Rela Geffen Monson conducted a statistical research project, "The Evolving Roles of American Congregational Rabbis," *Modern Judaism*, February (1982): pp. 73–89, which indicated that a rabbi's self-definition and priorities derive primarily from the needs of his/her congregation.

James S. Diamond and Jeremy Brochin, eds., *A Handbook for Hillel and Jewish Campus Professionals* (College Park, Maryland: Association of Hillel and Jewish Campus Professionals, 1983), offers insight into the world of Hillel and college campus work as seen by those currently engaged in the field. In addition to a generous dose of institutional information, this handbook contains noteworthy historical and sociological material.

In "Toward a New Generation of American Rabbis," *Reconstructionist*, XXXV (1969): pp. 7–14, Meir Ben-Horin examines the nature of the Reconstructionist rabbi, the philosophical infrastructure and the curriculum objectives of the Reconstructionist Rabbinical College.

The nature of rabbinic counseling is examined most completely in Earl Grollman, ed., *Rabbinical Counseling*, (New York: Bloch Publishing Co., 1966). Robert L. Katz analyzes the rabbi's pastoral role in *Pastoral Care and the Jewish Tradition* (Philadelphia: Fortress Press, 1984), and indirectly in *Empathy: Its Nature and Uses* (New York: Free Press of Glencoe, 1963). (He has also explored the therapeutic value of preaching in "Psychology and Preaching," *CCAR Journal* [June, 1955], and "The Rabbi as Preacher/Counselor. A Frame of Reference," *CCAR Journal* [June, 1958]). Steve L. Jacobs, "The Rabbi as Counselor: Reflections of a Neophyte," *CCAR Journal* (Winter, 1977): pp. 70–75; Perry London, "The Rabbi as Therapist," *Moment* (September, 1980): pp. 57–60; and Mortimer Ostow, "Pastoral Psychiatry," *Conservative Judaism* XXIII (1969): pp. 2–10, further explore the pastoral realm of rabbinic activity. (Ostow's article also describes the course in pastoral psychiatry offered by the Jewish Theological Seminary in the late '60s–early '70s. (Cf. Rochelle Endelman, "A Mental Health Educational Program for Rabbinical Students and Its Relevance to the Jewish Community," *Journal of Jewish Communal Service*, XLVI [1969]: pp. 176–184, which also describes the JTS program of study.)

Rabbinic hospital chaplaincy is considered in Adam S.

Fisher, "The Rabbinic Role and Practice in Visiting the Sick," *Journal of Reform Judaism* (Fall, 1982): pp. 43–55, and Arthur M. Oles, "The Chaplain as Rabbi," *CCAR Journal* (Winter, 1977): pp. 76–79. Mark H. Elovitz, "The Jewish Chaplaincy," *Tradition* 9 (1967): pp. 35–47, is an enlightening analysis of the difficulties facing rabbis considering a career in the military chaplaincy. Challenges confronting rabbis who serve on the college and university campus are assessed in Richard J. Israel, "The Rabbi on Campus," *Judaism* 16 (1967): pp. 186–192.

FICTION

Rabbi Philip Graetz, protagonist of Sidney L. Nyburg's *The Chosen People* (New York: Arno Press, 1975, © 1917), is probably the first Reform rabbi to appear in the pages of an American novel. Since then, rabbis have been regularly featured as characters in the literature of twentieth century American fiction. Many of these fictional rabbis function in a fashion that bears almost no similarity to activities of their colleagues in the real world. Yet some of these novels are based in fact, and properly considered, the fictional rabbis can serve to further understanding of the American rabbinate in specific and American Jewish life in general.

Murray Blackman, *A Guide to Jewish Themes in American Fiction, 1940–1980* (Metuchen, New Jersey: Scarecrow Press, 1981) is a wonderful resource that offers easy access to an array of Jewish topics treated in American fiction. Blackman's *Guide* contains brief précis of more than 1,600 novels as well as a cross-reference index to numerous Jewish themes. A thoughtful analysis of the image of the rabbi in American fiction is provided by Alan Ullman, "The Rabbi in American Jewish Fiction" (unpublished rabbinic thesis, Hebrew Union College–Institute of Religion, 1985).

Many of these novels portray self-righteous, crusading rabbis who struggle relentlessly to promote their cause despite much opposition and ambivalence from congregants. In

Israel Jacobs, *Ten For Kaddish* (New York: Norton, 1972), Rabbi Morris Kleinman's congregation disapproves of his insistence that anti-Semitism continues to threaten Jewish life in America. Reform Rabbi David Gordon, protagonist of Arkady Leokum's *The Temple* (New York: World Publishing Co., 1969), contends with a congregation opposed to his crusading. A rabbi's commitment to social action is of central concern in Howard Fast, *The Outsider*, (Boston: Houghton Mifflin, 1984).

Author Herbert Tarr, himself an ordained rabbi, is unsurpassed in finding the humorous (and often realistic) happenstances common to rabbinic work in America. His *Conversion of Chaplain Cohen* (New York: B. Geis Associates, dist. by Random House, 1963) and *Heaven Help Us* (New York: Random House, 1968) are comical portrayals peppered with enough realism to create engaging and enlightening reading. *Tell Me, Rabbi* by Morris N. Kertzer (New York: Bloch, 1976) similarly consists of a few dozen delightful vignettes, all "based on fact," which portray situations of humor and pathos in today's rabbinic endeavors. Harry Kemelman's Rabbi David Small experiences one adventure after the other while at the same time shedding some light on rabbinic work.

Rabbinic self-doubt and crisis of faith are also grist for the novelist's mill. The Orthodox rabbi in Mark Mirsky's *Blue Hill Avenue* (Indianapolis: The Bobbs Merrill Co., 1972) experiences a spiritual crisis when he is unable to explain the presence of irrational evil in the world. Noah Gordon, *The Rabbi* (New York: McGraw-Hill, 1965), depicts an idealistic rabbi who is sobered by a series of personal and professional failures.

SERMONS

Naomi W. Cohen's essay, "Sermons and the Contemporary World: Two American Jewish Sources," *Contemporary Jewry: Studies in Honor of Moshe Davis* (Jerusalem: 1984): pp. 23–44, underscores the historical significance of sermon collections; rabbinic homilies can add to our understanding of the contemporary rabbinate too.

The number of published (not to mention unpublished) sermon collections is too long to list. Many rabbis have had their sermons printed in a variety of forms (including the pages of temple bulletins), and congregations frequently publish their rabbi's finest sermons privately as a lasting tribute or memorial. Repositories like the American Jewish Archives in Cincinnati and the American Jewish Historical Society in Waltham, Massachusetts, preserve cartons of unpublished sermons—typed or written in longhand—among a rabbi's personal documents. This material constitutes a heretofore largely untapped resource for furthering our understanding of the rabbinate, both past and present.

APPENDIX B

SEMINARIES

Candidates seeking admission to rabbinical seminaries will find it helpful to write to the schools of their choice for further information and catalogs.

REFORM

Hebrew Union College–Jewish Institute of Religion
(HUC–JIR)
3101 Clifton Avenue
Cincinnati, OH 45220

Hebrew Union College–Jewish Institute of Religion
Brookdale Center
One West 4th Street
New York, NY 10012–1186

Hebrew Union College–Jewish Institute of Religion
3077 University Avenue
Los Angeles, CA 90007-3796

Hebrew Union College–Jewish Institute of Religion
13 King David Street
Jerusalem, Israel

RECONSTRUCTIONIST

The Reconstructionist Rabbinical College
Church Road & Greenwood Avenue
Wyncote, PA 19095

CONSERVATIVE

Jewish Theological Seminary (JTS)
3080 Broadway
New York, NY 10027

ORTHODOX

Yeshiva University
Rabbi Isaac Elchanan Theological Seminary (RIETS)
2540 Amsterdam Avenue
New York, NY 10033

Hebrew Theological College
7135 North Carpenter Road
Skokie, IL 60076

Central Yeshivah Beth
  Joseph Rabbinical Seminary
1427 49th Street
Brooklyn, NY 11219

Mesivta Yeshiva
Rabbi Chaim Berlin Rabbinical Academy
1593 Coney Island Avenue
Brooklyn, NY 11230

Mirrer Yeshivah Central Institute
1791–5 Ocean Parkway
Brooklyn, NY 11223

Ner Israel Rabbinical College
400 Mt. Wilson Lane
Baltimore, MD 21208

Rabbinical College of Telshe
28440 Euclid Avenue
Wickliffe, OH 44092

United Lubavitcher Yeshivoth
841–853 Ocean Parkway
Brooklyn, NY 11230

West Coast Talmudical Seminary
Mesivta Beth Midrash Elyon, Inc.
7215 Warring Street
Los Angeles, CA 90046

Yavneh Hebrew Theological Seminary
P.O.Box 185
Brooklyn, NY 11218

Yeshiva Torah Vodaath and Mesivta Rabbinical Seminary
425 East 9th Street
Brooklyn, NY 11218

ALLIED ORGANIZATIONS

B'nai B'rith Hillel Foundations, Inc.
2640 Rhode Island Avenue
Washington, DC 20036

Central Conference of American Rabbis (CCAR)
192 Lexington Avenue, Suite 701-2
New York, NY 10016

Jewish Reconstructionist Foundation
270 West 89th Street
New York, NY 10024

Rabbinical Alliance of America (Orthodox)
156 Fifth Avenue
New York, NY 10010

Rabbinical Assembly (RA) (Conservative)
3080 Broadway
New York, NY 10027

Rabbinical Council of America (RCA) (Orthodox)
275 Seventh Avenue
New York, NY 10001

Synagogue Council of America (Interdenominational)
327 Lexington Avenue
New York, NY 10016

Union of American Hebrew Congregations (UAHC)
(Reform)
838 Fifth Avenue
New York, NY 10021

Union of Orthodox Jewish Congregations of America
(UOJC)
45 West 36th Street
New York, NY 10018

Union of Orthodox Rabbis of the United States and
Canada
235 East Broadway
New York, NY 10002

The Federation of Reconstructionist Congregations and
Havurot
270 West 89th Street
New York, NY 10024

United Synagogue of America (USA) (Conservative)
3080 Broadway
New York, NY 10027

American Jewish Correctional Chaplains Association
10 East 73rd Street
New York, NY 10021

Jewish Chaplains Council (National Jewish Welfare
Board)
15 East 26th Street
New York, NY 10010

Appendix C

ABBREVIATIONS USED IN THIS BOOK

AHJCP	Association of Hillel and Jewish Campus Professionals
CCAR	Central Conference of American Rabbis
CSD	Community Service Division (Yeshiva University)
FRC	Federation of Reconstructionist Congregations
HUC-JIR	Hebrew Union College-Jewish Institute of Religion
JTS	Jewish Theological Seminary
JWB	Jewish Welfare Board
RIETS	Rabbi Isaac Elchanan Theological Seminary
RA	Rabbinical Assembly
RCA	Rabbinical Council of America
RRA	Reconstructionist Rabbinical Association
RRC	Reconstructionist Rabbinical College
UAHC	Union of American Hebrew Congregations
UOJC	Union of Orthodox Jewish Congregations
USA	United Synagogue of America

Index